What Readers Are Saying About the Fourth Edition of
Hello, Android

Once again, Ed has created a very smart guide for beginner and intermediate Android developers. It's a practical, highly readable guide whether you are just entering the world of Android application development, or if you have some experience but want to dive more deeply into concepts like basic game creation, animations, sound effects, threading, databases, and Google Play Services.

➤ **Diego Torres Milano**
Geek, Android system engineer, Linux advocate, and author

For a quick dip in the Android app development waters, it's tough to beat this updated version of the original book on the subject!

➤ **Mark Murphy**
Founder, CommonsWare and author of *The Busy Coder's Guide to Android Development*

Hello, Android concisely covers a lot of ground with engaging examples and an enjoyable writing style. I recommend this book to anyone who wants to ramp up quickly in Android development.

➤ **Jason Pike**
Software developer, theswiftlearner.com

The chapter on the Play Store was a wake-up call, showing how easy it is to get an app on there, in comparison with the fruity app store.

➤ **Stephen Wolff**
Director, Max Gate Digital Ltd.

Hello, Android

Introducing Google's Mobile Development Platform,
Fourth Edition

Ed Burnette

The Pragmatic Bookshelf

Dallas, Texas • Raleigh, North Carolina

Many of the designations used by manufacturers and sellers to distinguish their products are claimed as trademarks. Where those designations appear in this book, and The Pragmatic Programmers, LLC was aware of a trademark claim, the designations have been printed in initial capital letters or in all capitals. The Pragmatic Starter Kit, The Pragmatic Programmer, Pragmatic Programming, Pragmatic Bookshelf, PragProg and the linking *g* device are trademarks of The Pragmatic Programmers, LLC.

Every precaution was taken in the preparation of this book. However, the publisher assumes no responsibility for errors or omissions, or for damages that may result from the use of information (including program listings) contained herein.

Our Pragmatic courses, workshops, and other products can help you and your team create better software and have more fun. For more information, as well as the latest Pragmatic titles, please visit us at *https://pragprog.com*.

The Android robot is reproduced or modified from work created and shared by Google and used according to terms described in the Creative Commons 3.0 Attribution License.

The team that produced this book includes:

Susannah Davidson Pfalzer (editor)
Potomac Indexing, LLC (indexer)
Liz Welch (copyeditor)
Dave Thomas (typesetter)
Janet Furlow (producer)
Ellie Callahan (support)

For international rights, please contact *rights@pragprog.com*.

Printed in the United States of America.
ISBN-13: 978-1-68050-037-0
Printed on acid-free paper.
Book version: P1.0—May 2015

Contents

Part III — Thinking Outside the Box

Part IV — Beyond the Basics

Part V — Appendixes

Acknowledgments

I'd like to thank the many people who made this book possible, including the readers of the previous editions for all their great suggestions; my editor, Susannah Pfalzer, for her attention to detail; Craig Castelaz, Javier Collado, Eric Hung, Edward Ingram, Chris Johnson, Howard Koslow, Helen Li, Irakli Nadareishvili, Jan Nonnen, Jason Pike, Mike Riley, Sam Rose, Loren Sands-Ramshaw, Carlos Santana, Charley Stran, and Stephen Wolff for providing valuable review comments; and especially Lisa, Chris, and Michael, for their continued patience and support.

Preface

Android is an open source operating system for mobile phones and tablets that was created by Google and its partners and contributors. It's inside over a billion cell phones and other mobile devices, making Android the #1 platform for application developers. Whether you're a hobbyist or a professional programmer, whether you're doing it for fun or for profit, you need to learn more about developing for Android. This book will help you get started.

What Makes Android Special?

Many other mobile platforms are available on the market today, including iOS, Windows, Tizen, Firefox OS, and more. So why do people choose Android over the others? What's the difference?

Although some of its features have appeared before, Android is the first environment that combines the following:

- *An open, free development platform based on Linux and open source:* Handset makers like it because they can use and customize the platform without paying a royalty. Developers like it because they know that the platform "has legs" and is not locked into any one vendor that may go under or be acquired.

- *A component-based architecture inspired by Internet mashups:* Parts of one application can be used in ways not originally envisioned by the developer. You can even replace built-in components with your own improved versions. This has unleashed a new round of creativity in the mobile space.

- *Tons of services out of the box:* Location-based services use GPS or cell tower triangulation to allow you to customize the user experience depending on where you are. A full-powered SQL database lets you harness the power of local storage for occasionally connected computing and synchronization. Browser and map views can be embedded directly in your applications. All these capabilities help raise the bar on functionality while lowering your development costs.

- *Automatic management of the application life cycle:* Programs are isolated from each other by multiple layers of security, which provide a high level of system stability. The end user doesn't have to worry about what applications are active or close some programs so that others can run. Android is optimized for low-power, low-memory devices in a fundamental way that no previous platform has attempted.

- *High-quality graphics and sound:* Smooth, antialiased 2D and 3D-accelerated graphics have enabled new kinds of games and business applications. Codecs for the most common industry-standard audio and video formats are built right in, including H.264 (AVC), MP3, and AAC.

- *Portability across a wide range of current and future hardware:* All your programs are written in Java and executed by Android's ART ahead-of-time compiler or Dalvik virtual machine, so your code will be portable across ARM, x86, and other architectures. Support for a variety of input methods is included, such as keyboards, game pads, touch, TV remotes, mice, and trackballs. User interfaces can be customized for any screen resolution and orientation.

Android offers a fresh take on the way mobile applications interact with users, along with the technical underpinnings to make it possible. But the best part of Android is the software that you're going to write for it. This book will help you get off to a great start.

Who Should Read This Book?

This book is for developers new to the Android platform who are looking for a quick way to get started. In a just few minutes, you'll be installing the development tools and writing your first program. By the time you finish you'll be able to write complete, engaging Android applications. But more importantly, you'll be equipped to locate and understand more advanced material that you'll need in your journey.

Before tackling this book, you should understand the basic concepts of programming in Java, including classes, methods, scope, and inheritance. You'll also need to know the meaning of Java keywords such as import, static, final, public, and this. If you don't know what I'm talking about, then I recommend you start with a Java introductory book such as one of these:

- *Java Precisely [Ses05]*
- *Head First Java [SB05]*
- *Effective Java [Blo08]*
- *The Java Programming Language [AGH05]*
- *Java in a Nutshell [EF14]*

You don't need any prior experience developing software for mobile devices. In fact, if you do, it's probably best if you try to forget that experience. Android is so different that it's good to start with an open mind. However, some exposure to an integrated development environment (IDE) such as IntelliJ IDEA, Eclipse, or Visual Studio would come in handy.

What's in This Book?

Hello, Android is divided into four main parts. Roughly speaking, the book progresses from less advanced to more advanced topics, or from more common to less common aspects of Android.

Several chapters share a common example: an Android Ultimate Tic-Tac-Toe game. By gradually adding features to the game, you'll learn about many aspects of Android programming, including user interfaces, multimedia, and the Android Activity and Fragment life cycles.

In Part I, we'll start with an introduction to Android. This is where you'll learn how to install the Android emulator and how to use an IDE to write your first program. Then we'll introduce a few key concepts like the Android life cycle. Programming in Android is a little different from what you're probably used to, so make sure you get these concepts before moving on.

Part II talks about Android's user interface: display, input, multimedia, and animation. These features will be used in many of the programs you write.

Part III digs deeper into the Android platform. Here we'll explore making your app compatible with multiple Android devices and versions. You'll also learn how to publish your app on the Google Play Store.

Part IV wraps things up with a discussion of more advanced topics, including embedding HTML pages, accessing web services, using Google Play Services, and storing data with the built-in SQLite database.

At the end of the book, you'll find an appendix that covers the differences between Android and Java Standard Edition (SE), along with a bibliography.

What's New in the Fourth Edition?

The fourth edition has been updated to support all versions of Android from 4.1 through Android 5.1 and beyond. Version 4.1 (Jelly Bean) is the first of what I call the "modern" versions of Android.

What Came Before

Android 2.3 (Gingerbread) was the last of the old generation that worked only with phones. Version 3.0 (Honeycomb) was a major departure, but only supported tablets and saw limited adoption. (However, the Honeycomb statue at Google's campus is arguably the best.) 4.0 (Ice Cream Sandwich) combined the phone and tablet lines together like chocolate and vanilla but offered very little else in the way of functionality compared to 3.0.

New for Android 4.1 (Jelly Bean)

On the other hand, version 4.1 represented a major effort on Google's part to improve Android's usability and performance. Under the code name "Project Butter," Google added new ways to measure the speed and efficiency of the entire system, and then they optimized how each millisecond was used.[1]

New for Android 4.2 (Jelly Bean MR1)

Buoyed by the success of 4.1, Google decided to keep the same name for the next two releases. Version 4.2 continued performance improvements, added multiuser support, and included the ability to wirelessly mirror your screen to a remote display using the Miracast standard.[2]

New for Android 4.3 (Jelly Bean MR2)

The focus of version 4.3 was security. SE (Security Enhanced) Linux was used as the underlying operating system, and restricted profiles allowed different users to have different permissions set up by the primary owner. This version also was the first to include support for OpenGL ES 3.0.[3]

---

1. http://d.android.com/sdk/api_diff/16/changes.html
2. http://d.android.com/sdk/api_diff/17/changes.html
3. http://d.android.com/sdk/api_diff/18/changes.html

New for Android 4.4 (KitKat)

The most important new feature in Android 4.4 was the replacement of the old WebKit-based WebView with the Chromium engine, the same one used in the Chrome browser.[4]

New for Android 4.4W (KitKat for Watches)

Android Wear, the operating system for smart watches, required a few changes and fixes to support wearable devices.[5]

New for Android 5.0 (Lollipop)

A new design language called "Material Design" was the most visible change in Android 5.0. Under the covers, the Dalvik VM that was used on every version of Android up to this point was replaced by a system called ART, which relied on ahead-of-time compilation to get better performance. Finally, a new effort called "Project Volta" was started to do the same for battery life that Project Butter did for performance.[6]

New for Android 5.1 (Lollipop MR1)

Support for multiple SIM cards was added, as well as a way for carrier provisioning apps to be distributed through Google Play. In addition, the AndroidHttpClient class and a large number of org.apache.http classes were deprecated.[7]

If I remember my alphabet correctly, after L comes M, N, O, and P (or "eleminopea" as I was taught to sing it). If you follow the advice in this book, your programs will run on future versions of Android with little or no effort. Chapter 8, *Write Once, Test Everywhere*, on page 113 covers how to create a single program that supports multiple versions.

See the Android Device Dashboard[8] for the latest market share of active Android devices in the wild. All the examples in this book have been tested on versions 4.1 through 5.1.

This edition of the book doesn't cover versions earlier than 4.1 because they represent a small and shrinking portion of the market. Nor does it spend much time on the customizations possible in 5.1 since there aren't many

---

4. http://d.android.com/sdk/api_diff/19/changes.html
5. http://d.android.com/sdk/api_diff/20/changes.html
6. http://d.android.com/sdk/api_diff/21/changes.html
7. http://d.android.com/sdk/api_diff/22/changes.html
8. http://d.android.com/resources/dashboard/platform-versions.html

devices running that version as of this writing. Only the topics needed by most Android programs are included to keep the book short and concise.

Online Resources

At the website for this book[9], you'll find the following:

- The full source code for all the sample programs used in this book, along with resources such as sounds and images

- An errata page, listing any mistakes in the current edition (let's hope that will be empty!)

- A discussion forum where you can communicate directly with the author and other Android developers (let's hope that will be full!)

You're free to use the source code in your own applications as you see fit. Note: If you're reading the ebook, you can also click the little rectangle before the code listings to download that source file directly.

Fast-Forward >>

Although most authors expect you to read every word in their books, I know you're not going to do that. You want to read just enough to let you get something done, and then maybe you'll come back later and read something else to let you get another piece done. So, I've tried to provide you with a little help so you won't get lost.

Each chapter in this book ends with a "Fast-Forward >>" section. These sections will provide some guidance for where you should go next when you need to read the book out of order. You'll also find pointers to other resources such as books and online documentation here in case you want to learn more about the subject.

So, what are you waiting for? The next chapter—Chapter 1, *Quick Start*, on page 3—gets you started with a very simple Android program. Chapter 2, *Key Concepts*, on page 15 takes a step back and introduces you to the basic concepts and philosophy of Android, and Chapter 3, *Opening Moves*, on page 31 introduces the Tic-Tac-Toe example and digs into the user interface, which will be the most important part of most Android programs.

Your ultimate goal will be to make your apps available for sale or free download in the Android Market. When you're ready, Chapter 9, *Publishing to the Play Store*, on page 125 will show you how to take that final step.

---

9.   http://pragprog.com/book/eband4

Part I

Introducing Android

CHAPTER 1

Quick Start

Android combines the ubiquity of cell phones, the excitement of open source software, and the corporate backing of Google and other Open Handset Alliance members such as Samsung, HTC, China Mobile, Verizon, and AT&T. The result is a mobile platform you can't afford *not* to learn.

Luckily, getting started developing with Android is easy. You don't even need access to an Android phone—just a computer where you can install the Android SDK and device emulator.

In this chapter, I'll show you how to get all the development tools installed, and then we'll jump right in and create a working application: Android's version of "Hello, World." If you're not an Android beginner, feel free to skim this chapter or skip it completely and go to Chapter 2, *Key Concepts*, on page 15.

Installing the Tools

The Android software development kit (SDK) works on Windows, Linux, and Mac OS X. The applications you create, of course, can be deployed on any Android device.

Before you start coding, you need to install Java, an IDE, and the Android SDK.

Java Development Kit (JDK) 7.0+

First you need a copy of Java. All the Android development tools require it, and programs you write will be using the Java language. JDK 7 or 8 is required.

Note: Mac users can skip this part. Android Studio will automatically install the right version of Java if you don't have it. However, there have been reports of problems with mismatched Java versions on the Mac. If you get errors, you can find troubleshooting tips[1] at the Stack Overflow website.[2]

It's not enough to just have a runtime environment (JRE); you need the full development kit. I recommend getting the latest Java SE 8 JDK update from the Oracle download site.[3]

You should also set your JAVA_HOME environment variable to point to the location where you installed the JDK. The exact way that you do this depends on your operating system version. For example, on Windows 7 you click the Start button, right-click on Computer, select Properties, and then click "Advanced system settings." Click Environment Variables..., and under the list of system variables click New.... Enter the variable name "JAVA_HOME" without the quotes, and enter the directory where you installed the JDK as the value. Click OK to close all the windows and save the setting.

To verify you have the right version, run these commands from a new shell window. (To open a shell window on Windows, click the Start button, type cmd, and press Enter.) Here's what I get when I run them:

```
C:\> java -version
java version "1.8.0_31"
Java(TM) SE Runtime Environment (build 1.8.0_31-b13)
Java HotSpot(TM) 64-Bit Server VM (build 25.31-b07, mixed mode)

C:\> echo %JAVA_HOME%
C:\Program Files\Java\jdk1.8.0_31
```

You should see something similar, with version "1.7.something" or later.

Android Studio

Next, you should install a Java development environment if you don't have one already. I recommend Android Studio, because it's free and because it's used and supported by the Google developers who created Android.

You should always use whatever is the most up-to-date beta or production version. Go to the Android Studio downloads page,[4] and click the Download Android Studio button.

Note: If you don't want to use Android Studio (there's always one in every crowd), support for other IDEs such as NetBeans and Eclipse is available

1. http://stackoverflow.com/questions/16636146
2. http://stackoverflow.com/questions/24472020
3. http://www.oracle.com/technetwork/java/javase/downloads
4. http://d.android.com/sdk

from their respective communities. Or if you're really old-school, you can forgo an IDE entirely and just use the command-line tools.[5] The rest of the book will assume you're using Android Studio, so if you're not, you'll need to make adjustments as necessary.

What Happened to Eclipse?

Until recently, most Android developers used the Eclipse IDE[a] and the Android Development Tools. In May 2013, Google introduced Android Studio, a new development environment based on IntelliJ IDEA by JetBrains.[b]

The biggest change in Android Studio is its use of the Gradle system for builds. Android Studio also has a number of new features such as a much improved WYSIWYG editor and the ability to use the same code to build multiple configurations. Eclipse is still supported, but most new development will be done in Android Studio.

---

a.   http://www.eclipse.org
b.   http://www.jetbrains.com/idea

Once you've downloaded the install program, start it and follow the instructions on the screen. Accept the standard default values for everything, and just keep clicking the Next or Finish button. It may take several minutes to download and install everything you need. Eventually you'll see the following:

This means you have installed Android Studio successfully and are ready to start development.

Keep in mind that Android Studio is constantly evolving, so you may see slightly different screens than the ones in this book. New versions may even change default filenames and directories. Please adjust your actions accordingly and report any discrepancies on the online forum for the book.[6]

Whew! Luckily, you have to do that only once. Now that everything is installed, it's time to write your first program.

Creating Your First Program

Android Studio comes with several built-in example programs, or templates. We're going to use one of them to create a simple "Hello, Android" program in just a few seconds. Get your stopwatch ready. Ready? Set? Go!

Select "Start a new Android Studio project" to open the New Project dialog box.

You'll see a series of four screens. The first one asks for the application name and location:

Enter "Hello Android" for the application name and "example.org" for the company domain. Android Studio will fill in the rest. Click Next to continue.

The second screen prompts for the version of Android to target:

---

6. http://pragprog.com/book/eband4

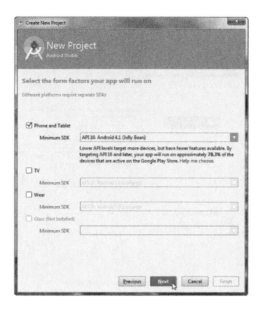

Select "Phone and Tablet" and specify the Minimum SDK as "API 16: Android 4.1 (Jelly Bean)." This is a very important step, so verify that you have the right version selected. Then click Next.

The third screen asks you to select the type of example activity to add:

Select "Blank Activity with Fragment" and click Next.

The last screen asks for the activity name and other information:

Change Activity Name to "HelloActivity" and the rest will be filled in.

To save time in the future, for the other examples in this book we'll use a shorthand notation like the following to indicate all these New Project values:

```
Application name: Hello Android
Company Domain: example.org
Form factors: Phone and Tablet
Minimum SDK: API 16: Android 4.1 (Jelly Bean)
Add activity: Blank Activity with Fragment
Activity Name: HelloActivity
```

After you fill out the last screen, click Finish. The IDE creates the project and fills it in with some default files. Then the IDE builds it and packages it up so it's ready to execute.

Note: If you get an error message about "Rendering Problems" in the editor for fragment_hello.xml, just close the window and ignore it. It's a known bug in Android Studio.

OK, the wizard takes care of writing the program so now all that's left is to try running it. First let's run it under the Android emulator.

Running on the Android Emulator

An emulator is a program that mimics one kind of hardware while running on a different kind of hardware. With the Android emulator, you can create a virtual version of just about any tablet, phone, or wearable right on your desktop.

To run your Android program, select Run > Run 'app' or click the Run button on the toolbar:

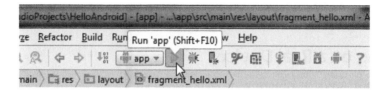

In a few moments the Choose Device window will open:

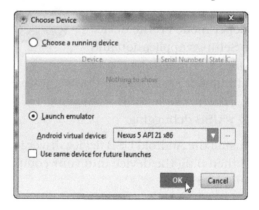

Verify that "Launch emulator" is selected and that the name of an Android virtual device (AVD) has been filled in. Click OK to run it.

The Android emulator window will now start up and boot the Android operating system. The first time you do this, it may take minute or two, so be patient. If you see a key guard screen, swipe it as directed to unlock.

Android Studio sends a copy of your program to the emulator to execute. The application screen comes up, and your "Hello, Android" program is now running (see the following figure).

(If the emulator didn't appear after a few minutes or appeared to hang, your computer may not be compatible with Intel's hardware acceleration. Create a new AVD and specify the ARM processor instead of Intel x86. See *Gentlemen, Start Your Emulators*, on page 114 for more information. Another option is to use the Genymotion emulator.[7])

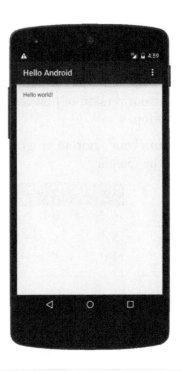

That's it! Congratulations on your first Android program.

Running on a Real Device

Running an Android program on a physical device such as the Nexus 5 during development is almost identical to running it on the emulator. On Android 4.2 and above, you need to enable developer mode on the device itself by starting the Settings application and selecting "About phone" or "About tablet" and tapping on the Build number seven times (that's a little Easter egg from the Android developers). Then enable USB debugging by selecting Developer options > Debugging > USB debugging.

On your computer, install the Android USB device driver if you haven't already (Windows only), and then plug the device into your computer using the USB cable that came with the unit.

Getting the USB driver running for the first time can be tricky. See the Using Hardware Devices page[8] for the latest device driver and installation instructions. If you get a message asking you to allow USB debugging, along with your computer's RSA key fingerprint, check the box that says "Always allow from this computer" and then select OK.

The next time you run the app, the device will appear in the Choose Device window. You can have several emulators and devices running at once and choose between them each time, or you can check the "Use same device for future launches" option. If your device does not appear in the list, it usually

---

7. http://www.genymotion.com
8. http://d.android.com/tools/device.html

indicates a problem with your USB driver or the version of Android you're targeting.

When you're ready to publish your application for others to use, you'll need to take few more steps. Chapter 9, *Publishing to the Play Store*, on page 125 will cover that in more detail.

Shortening the Turnaround

Starting the emulator is expensive. Think about it this way—when you first turn on your phone, it needs to boot up just like any computer system. Closing the emulator is just like turning off the phone or pulling the batteries out. So, don't turn it off!

Leave the emulator window running as long as Android Studio is running. The next time you start an Android program, Android Studio will notice the emulator is already there and will just send it the new program to run.

Additional Steps

We skipped a couple of steps to get things running quickly. Let's go over them now.

Checking for Updates

Android Studio is a work in progress that changes much more often than the Android SDK. The version you download may be different from the one I used when writing this book, and it may contain a few, shall we say, idiosyncrasies.

For this reason, I recommend you allow the IDE to automatically check for updates, and download and install new updates as soon as they're available. You can also select Help > Check for Update to perform a manual check at any time.

Adding SDK Packages

The Android Studio installer includes the Android SDK and tools needed for initial development. However, as you progress, you may find that you need more than the minimum. To get that, you'll need to run the Android SDK Manager.

In Android Studio, select Tools > Android > SDK Manager. The Manager displays a list of available components, including documentation, platforms, add-on libraries, and USB drivers, as shown in the following figure.

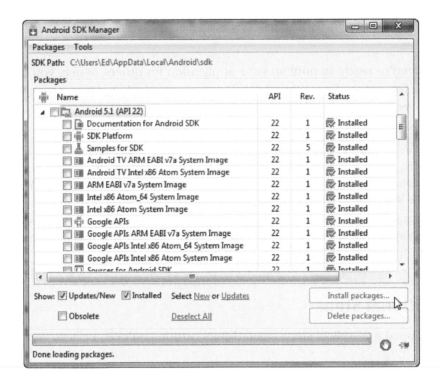

I recommend installing the most recent version of these items:

Android SDK Tools
Software development kit

Android SDK Platform-tools
Low-level tools like adb (Android Debug Bridge)

Android SDK Build-tools
Required for building

Android 5.1 (API 22) (or later)
Install all components for the highest version available

Under the Extras category, install these if they're not already installed:

Android Support Repository
Needed by gradle

Android Support Library
For compatibility with older Android versions

Google Play services
Value-added library that contains many nice features

Google Repository
    Needed by gradle

Google USB Driver (Windows only)
    Allows you to run and debug programs on real devices

Intel x86 Emulator Accelerator
    Add-on package to make the emulator faster

Once you've selected everything you want to install, click the Install button. This can take a long time to complete. If you're prompted to accept the license agreements, be sure to accept each different license (sometimes there are more than one). And if you get a message about restarting the SDK Manager, allow it to proceed. If you get an HTTPS SSL error, then select Tools > Options from the Android SDK Manager window and select the "Force https:// sources to be fetched using http://" option.

Fast-Forward >>

Thanks to Android Studio, creating a skeletal Android program takes only a few seconds. In Chapter 3, *Opening Moves*, on page 31, we'll begin to flesh out that skeleton with a real application—a Tic-Tac-Toe game. This sample will be used in several chapters to demonstrate Android's API.

But before delving into that, you should take a few minutes to read Chapter 2, *Key Concepts*, on page 15. Once you grasp the basic concepts such as activities and life cycles, the rest will be much easier to understand.

Although the use of Android Studio to develop Android programs is optional, I highly recommend it. If you've never used IntelliJ before, you may want to invest some time reading the IntelliJ IDEA Quick Start guides at the JetBrains website.[9] Pay particular attention to the keyboard shortcuts, because learning just a few of those will save you a lot of time.

---

9.   http://www.jetbrains.com/idea/documentation

CHAPTER 2

Key Concepts

Now that you have an idea of what Android is, let's take a look at how it works. Some parts of Android may be familiar, such as the Linux kernel and the SQL database. Others will be completely foreign, such as Android's idea of the application life cycle.

You'll need a good understanding of these key concepts in order to write well-behaved Android applications, so if you read only one chapter in this book, read this one.

The Big Picture

Let's start by taking a look at the overall system architecture—the key layers and components that make up the Android open source software stack. In the figure on page 16, you can see the "20,000-foot" view of Android. Study it closely—there will be a test tomorrow.

Each layer uses the services provided by the layers below it. Starting from the bottom, the following sections highlight the layers provided by Android.

Linux Kernel

Android is built on top of a solid and proven foundation: the Linux kernel. Created by Linus Torvalds in 1991, Linux can be found today in everything from wristwatches to supercomputers. Linux provides the hardware abstraction layer for Android, allowing Android to be ported to a wide variety of platforms in the future.

Internally, Android uses Linux for its memory management, process management, networking, and other operating system services. The Android user will never see Linux, and your programs will not usually make Linux calls directly. As a developer, though, you'll need to be aware it's there.

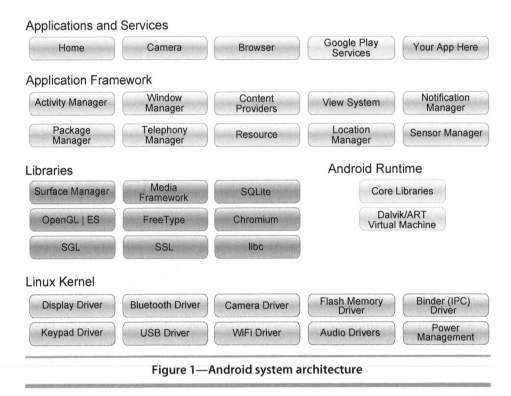

Figure 1—Android system architecture

Some utilities you need during development interact with Linux. For example, the adb shell command[1] will open a Linux shell in which you can enter other commands to run on the device. From there you can examine the Linux file system, view active processes, and so forth, subject to security restrictions.

Native Libraries

The next layer above the kernel contains the Android native libraries. These shared libraries are all written in C or C++, compiled for the particular hardware architecture used by the Android device, and preinstalled by the vendor.

Some of the most important native libraries include the following:

- *Surface Manager*: Instead of drawing directly to the screen, your drawing commands are saved into lists that are then combined with lists from other windows and are then composited to form the display the user sees. This lets the system create all sorts of interesting effects, such as see-through windows and fancy transitions.

---

1. http://d.android.com/tools/help/adb.html

- *2D and 3D graphics*: Two- and three-dimensional elements can be combined in a single user interface with Android. Everything is converted into 3D drawing lists and rendered by hardware for the fastest possible experience.

- *Media codecs*: Android can play video and record and play back audio in various formats, including AAC, AVC (H.264), H.263, MP3, and MPEG-4.

- *SQL database*: Android includes the lightweight SQLite database engine,[2] the same database used in Firefox and the Apple iPhone. You can use this for persistent storage in your application.

- *Browser engine*: For the fast display of HTML content, Android uses the Chromium library.[3] This is the same engine used in the Google Chrome browser, and it's a close cousin of the one used in Apple's Safari browser and the Apple iPhone.

These libraries aren't applications that stand by themselves. They exist only to be called by higher-level programs. You can write and deploy your own native libraries using the Native Development Toolkit (NDK). Native development is beyond the scope of this book, but if you're interested, you can read all about it online.[4]

Android Runtime

Also sitting on top of the kernel is the Android runtime, including the runtime environment and the core Java libraries. Depending on the version of Android, the environment uses either Dalvik or ART.

Dalvik is a virtual machine (VM) designed and written by Dan Bornstein at Google. Your code gets compiled into machine-independent instructions called *bytecodes*, which are then executed by the Dalvik VM on the mobile device.

ART (Android Runtime) is an ahead-of-time compiler that replaced Dalvik in Android 5.0 (Lollipop). When an application is installed onto your Android device, ART compiles it into machine code. Compared to Dalvik, this makes programs run faster at the expense of a longer install time.

Dalvik and ART are Google's semi-compatible implementation of Java, optimized for mobile devices. All the code you write for Android will be written in Java and run by Dalvik or ART.

---

2. http://www.sqlite.org
3. http://www.chromium.org
4. http://d.android.com/tools/sdk/ndk

Note that the core Java libraries that come with Android are different from both the Java Standard Edition (Java SE) libraries and the Java Mobile Edition (Java ME) libraries. A substantial amount of overlap exists, however. In Appendix 1, *Java vs. the Android Language and APIs*, on page 207, you'll find a comparison of Android and standard Java libraries.

Application Framework

Sitting above the native libraries and runtime, you'll find the Application Framework layer. This layer provides the high-level building blocks you'll use to create your applications. The framework comes preinstalled with Android, but you can also extend it with your own components as needed.

Embrace and Extend

One of the unique and powerful qualities of Android is that all applications have a level playing field. What I mean is that the system applications have to go through the same public API that you use. You can even tell Android to make your application replace the standard applications if you want.

The most important parts of the framework are as follows:

- *Activity manager:* This controls the life cycle of applications (see *It's Alive!*, on page 22) and maintains a common "backstack" for user navigation.

- *Content providers:* These objects encapsulate data that needs to be shared between applications, such as contacts. See *Content Providers*, on page 21.

- *Resource manager:* Resources are anything that goes with your program that is not code. See *Using Resources*, on page 21.

- *Location manager:* An Android device always knows where it is. See Chapter 12, *Using Google Play Services*, on page 169.

- *Notification manager:* Events such as arriving messages, appointments, proximity alerts, alien invasions, and more can be presented in an unobtrusive fashion to the user.

Applications and Services

The highest layer in the Android architecture diagram is the Applications and Services layer. Think of this as the tip of the Android iceberg. End users will see only the applications, blissfully unaware of all the action going on below the waterline. As the developer, however, you know better.

Applications are programs that can take over the whole screen and interact with the user. On the other hand, services operate invisibly to extend the application framework. The majority of this book will cover application development, because that's what most of you will be writing.

When someone buys an Android phone or tablet, it will come prepackaged with a number of standard system applications, including the following:

- Phone dialer
- Email
- Camera
- Web browser
- Google Play Store

Using the Play Store, users will be able to download new programs to run on their phone. That's where you come in. By the time you finish this book, you'll be able to write your own awesome applications for Android.

The Android framework provides a number of building blocks that you use to create your applications. Let's take a look at those next.

Building Blocks

A few objects are defined in the Android SDK that every developer needs to be familiar with. The most important ones are activities, fragments, views, intents, services, and content providers. You'll see examples of most of these in the rest of the book, so I'd like to briefly introduce them now.

Activities

An *activity* is a user interface screen. Applications can define one or more activities to handle different phases of the program. As discussed in *It's Alive!*, on page 22, each activity is responsible for saving its own state so that it can be restored later as part of the application life cycle. See *Creating the Main Screen*, on page 33 for an example. Activities extend the Context class, so you can use them to get global information about your application.

Fragments

A *fragment* is a component of an activity. Usually they're displayed on the screen, but they don't have to be. Fragments were introduced in Android 3.0 (Honeycomb), but if you need to target older versions of Android you can use a compatibility library.

If you consider an email program, there's one part of the app that displays the list of all the mail you have, and another part that displays the text of one email. These could be (and probably are) implemented as two different fragments. Using fragments allows you to more easily adapt to different-sized screens (see the following diagram).

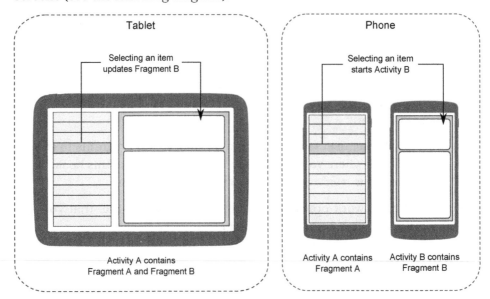

Views

A *view* is the smallest level of the user interface. Views are contained directly by activities or by fragments inside activities. They can be created by Java code, or preferably, by XML layouts. Each view has a series of attributes, or properties, that control what it does, how it acts, and what it displays.

Intents

An *intent* is a mechanism for describing a specific action, such as "pick a photo," "phone home," or "open the pod bay doors." In Android, just about everything goes through intents, so you have plenty of opportunities to replace or reuse components. See *Browsing by Intent*, on page 138 for an example of an intent.

For example, there's an intent for "send an email." If your application needs to send mail, you can invoke that intent. Or if you're writing a new email application, you can register an activity to handle that intent and replace the standard mail program. The next time somebody tries to send an email, that person will get the option to use your program instead of the standard one.

Services

A *service* is a task that runs in the background without the user's direct interaction, similar to a Unix daemon. For example, consider a music player. The music may be started by an activity, but you want it to keep playing even when the user has moved on to a different program. So, the code that does the actual playing should be in a service. Later, another activity may bind to that service and tell it to switch tracks or stop playing.

Android comes with many services built in, along with convenient APIs to access them. Google also provides optional services for extra functionality (see Chapter 12, *Using Google Play Services*, on page 169).

Content Providers

A *content provider* is a set of data wrapped up in a custom API to read and write it. This is the best way to share global data *between applications*. For example, Google provides a content provider for contacts. All the information there—names, addresses, phone numbers, and so forth—can be shared by any application that wants to use it. See *Using a ContentProvider*, on page 196 for an example.

Using Resources

A *resource* is a localized text string, bitmap, or other small piece of noncode information that your program needs. At build time all your resources get compiled into your application. This is useful for internationalization and for supporting multiple device types (see *Specifying Alternate Resources*, on page 120).

You'll create and store your resources in the res directory inside your project. The Android resource compiler (aapt)[5] processes resources according to which subfolder they're in and the format of the file. For example, PNG and JPG format bitmaps should go in a directory starting with res/drawable, and XML files that describe screen layouts should go in a directory starting with res/layout. You can add suffixes for particular languages, screen orientations, pixel densities, and more (see *All Screens Great and Small*, on page 119).

The resource compiler compresses and packs your resources and then generates a class named R that contains identifiers you use to reference those resources in your program. This is a little different from standard Java resources, which are referenced by key strings. Doing it this way allows

---

5. http://d.android.com/tools/building

Android to make sure all your references are valid and saves space by not having to store all those resource keys. We'll see an example of the code to access a resource in Chapter 3, *Opening Moves*, on page 31.

Now let's take a closer look at the life cycle of an Android application. It's a little different from what you're used to seeing.

It's Alive!

On your standard Linux or Windows desktop, you can have many applications running and visible at once in different windows. One of the windows has keyboard focus, but otherwise all the programs are equal. You can easily switch between them, but it's your responsibility as the user to move the windows around so you can see what you're doing and close programs you don't need.

Android doesn't work that way.

In Android, there's one foreground application, which typically takes over the whole display except for the status line. When users turn on their phone or tablet, the first application they see is the Home application (see the figure).

When the user runs an application, Android starts it and brings it to the foreground. From that application, the user might invoke another application, or another screen in the same application, and then another and another. All these programs and screens are recorded on the *application stack* by the system's Activity Manager. At any time, users can press the Back button to return to the previous screen on the stack. From the users' point of view, it works a lot like the history in a web browser. Pressing Back returns them to the previous page.

Process != Application

Internally, each user interface screen is represented by an Activity class (see *Activities*, on page 19). Each activity has its own life cycle. An application is one or more activities plus a Linux process to contain them. That sounds pretty straightforward, doesn't it? But don't get comfortable yet; I'm about to throw you a curve ball.

In Android, an application can be "alive" even if its process has been killed. Put another way, the activity life cycle isn't tied to the process life cycle. Processes are just disposable containers for activities.

Life Cycles of the Rich and Famous

During its lifetime, each activity of an Android program can be in one of several states, as shown in the following figure. You, the developer, don't have control over what state your program is in. That's all managed by the system. However, you do get notified when the state is about to change through the on*XX*() method calls.

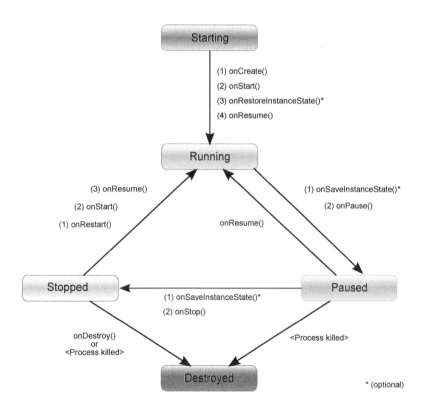

You override these methods in your Activity class, and Android will call them at the appropriate time:

- onCreate(Bundle): This is called when the activity first starts up. You can use it to perform one-time initialization such as creating the user interface. onCreate() takes one parameter that is either null or some state information previously saved by the onSaveInstanceState() method.

- onStart(): This indicates the activity is about to be displayed to the user.

- onResume(): This is called when your activity can start interacting with the user. This is a good place to start animations and music.

- onPause(): This runs when the activity is about to go into the background, usually because another activity has been launched in front of it. This is where you should save your program's persistent state, such as a database record being edited.

- onStop(): This is called when your activity is no longer visible to the user and it won't be needed for a while. If memory is tight, onStop() may never be called (the system may simply terminate your process).

- onRestart(): If this method is called, it indicates your activity is being redisplayed to the user from a stopped state.

- onDestroy(): This is called right before your activity is destroyed. If memory is tight, onDestroy() may never be called (the system may simply terminate your process).

- onSaveInstanceState(Bundle): Android will call this method to allow the activity to save per-instance state, such as a cursor position within a text field. Usually you won't need to override it because the default implementation saves the state for all your user interface controls automatically.

- onRestoreInstanceState(Bundle): This is called when the activity is being reinitialized from a state previously saved by the onSaveInstanceState() method. The default implementation restores the state of your user interface.

Activities that aren't running in the foreground may be stopped, or the Linux process that houses them may be killed at any time in order to make room for new activities. This will be a common occurrence, so it's important that your application be designed from the beginning with this in mind. In some cases, the onPause() method may be the last method called in your activity, so that's where you should save any data you want to keep around for next time.

Starting with Android 3.0 (Honeycomb), Google introduced another twist in the story of application life cycles: *fragments*.

Better Living Through Fragments

Fragments represent a component of your application. They're contained within activities (see *Fragments*, on page 19). and have a life cycle very similar to activities. In fact, many of the life-cycle methods for fragments are called by the methods of the Activity (for example, Fragment.onResume() is called indirectly by Activity.onResume()). See the following diagram for details:

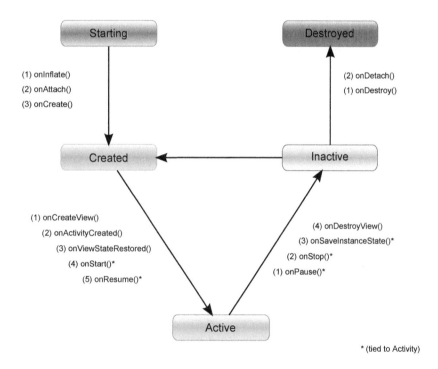

Fragments can outlive the activities that contain them. For example, if you rotate the screen while an app is running, the activity will usually be destroyed and re-created so that it can adjust to the new screen dimensions. However, the fragments will usually keep on going. This lets you keep heavyweight objects such as a network connection alive during the transition.

Safe and Secure

As mentioned earlier, every application runs in its own Linux process. The hardware forbids one process from accessing another process's memory. Furthermore, every application is assigned a specific user ID. Any files it creates cannot be read or written by other applications as long as the device hasn't been "rooted" (modified to run apps with elevated privileges).

In addition, access to certain critical operations is restricted, and you must specifically ask for permission to use them in a file named AndroidManifest.xml. When the application is installed, the Package Manager either grants or doesn't grant the permissions based on certificates and, if necessary, user prompts. Here are some of the most common permissions you'll need:

- INTERNET: Access the Internet.

- READ_CONTACTS: Read (but don't write) the user's contacts data.

- WRITE_CONTACTS: Write (but don't read) the user's contacts data.

- RECEIVE_SMS: Monitor incoming SMS (text) messages.

- ACCESS_COARSE_LOCATION: Use a coarse location provider such as cell towers or Wi-Fi.

- ACCESS_FINE_LOCATION: Use a more accurate location provider such as GPS.

For example, to monitor incoming SMS messages you'd specify this in the manifest file:

```
<manifest xmlns:android="http://schemas.android.com/apk/res/android"
    package="com.google.android.app.myapp" >
    <uses-permission android:name="android.permission.RECEIVE_SMS" />
</manifest>
```

Android can even restrict access to entire parts of the system. Using XML tags in AndroidManifest.xml, you can restrict who can start an activity, start or bind to a service, broadcast intents to a receiver, or access the data in a content provider. This additional level of control is beyond the scope of this book, but if you want to learn more, read the online help for the Android security model.[6]

---

6.   http://d.android.com/training/articles/security-tips.html

Fast-Forward >>

The rest of this book will use all the concepts introduced in this chapter. In Chapter 3, *Opening Moves*, on page 31, we'll use activities and life-cycle methods to define a sample application. Media codecs will be explored in Chapter 6, *Adding Sounds*, on page 93, and content providers will be covered in Chapter 13, *Putting SQL to Work*, on page 183.

Part II

Let's Play a Game

CHAPTER 3

Opening Moves

In Chapter 1, *Quick Start*, on page 3, we used Android Studio to put together a simple "Hello, Android" program in a few minutes. Like most platypuses, that program doesn't do much. In Part II, we'll create a much more interesting application, a game of Ultimate Tic-Tac-Toe.

By gradually adding more functionality to the program you'll learn about many different aspects of Android programming. This knowledge will help you later with your own programs, whether they're games, business apps, or anything else you can imagine. We'll start with the user interface.

Each example in this book is printed in its entirety so you can follow along in Android Studio as you read. However, you can save yourself a lot of typing by downloading the examples from the book's website.[1] If you're reading the ebook version of this book, you can click the filename before the code listings to download that file directly.

Creating the Tic-Tac-Toe Example

Everybody knows how to play Tic-Tac-Toe: a 3×3 array of tiles, initially empty, is filled in by two players who mark either an X or an O in an empty spot. The first player to get three of their marks in a row wins. If the board fills up first, then that's a tie and nobody wins.

Ultimate Tic-Tac-Toe[2] is similar, except that you can't simply put a mark in your square—you have to win the square by playing a nested game of Tic-Tac-Toe using a 3×3 array of smaller tiles inside the big one. See the figure on page 32 for an example.

---

1. http://pragprog.com/book/eband4
2. http://mathwithbaddrawings.com/2013/06/16/ultimate-tic-tac-toe

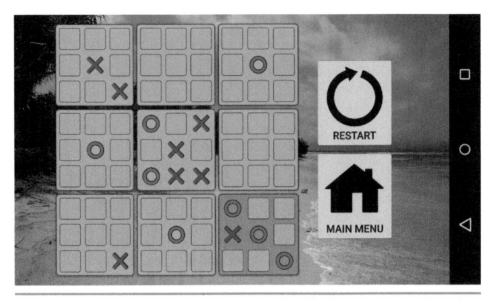

Figure 2—Tic-Tac-Toe meets Inception

There are many variations, but we're going to use the one where a tie in the small game makes the big tile count for both players. The rules are similar to the popular Android and iOS game Tic Tactics.[3] (Note that I don't have any relationship with the makers of Tic Tactics, but if I hadn't spent so much time playing their game, I might have finished this book a year earlier.)

To create the new program, select File > New Project and enter the following information:

```
Application name: Tic Tac Toe
Company Domain: example.org
Form factors: Phone and Tablet
Minimum SDK: API 16: Android 4.1 (Jelly Bean)
Add activity: Blank Activity
Activity Name: MainActivity
Layout Name: activity_main
Title: UT3
```

You can delete the res/menu directory because we won't be needing it for this project.

Before we get into the actual game part of the program, we need to design a starting screen. We do this by editing a layout file in XML.

---

3. http://www.hiddenvariable.com/tictactics/

Designing in XML

There are two ways to define a user interface in Android: in code, or in XML. XML is usually recommended because it's easier to create and style than the equivalent Java code.

Android Studio has a graphical layout editor to help you create beautiful user interfaces by dragging and dropping components such as buttons and lists onto a canvas, and then positioning them with your mouse. You should play around with the editor and use it whenever you like, but for this book we're just going to work with the XML text that it creates. This will give you a better feel for how things work.

Creating the Main Screen

When users start the program, we want to show options for continuing a game, starting a new game, and for reading about what the program does. The following figure shows the screen we want to design.

To create this screen, edit the activity_main.xml file by going to Android Studio's Project window and double-clicking on the filename under the res/layout folder. (Note that the Project window can be in one of three modes: Project, Packages, and Android. You can change the mode by selecting the drop-down menu next to the window name.)

Select the Text tab at the bottom of the editor window if you don't see the XML. Change the text to this:

```
ticTacToev1/src/main/res/layout/activity_main.xml
<FrameLayout
    xmlns:android="http://schemas.android.com/apk/res/android"
    xmlns:tools="http://schemas.android.com/tools"
    android:layout_width="match_parent"
    android:layout_height="match_parent"
    android:clipChildren="false"
    tools:context=".TicTacToeActivity">

    <fragment
        android:id="@+id/main_fragment"
        class="org.example.tictactoe.MainFragment"
        android:layout_width="wrap_content"
        android:layout_height="wrap_content"
        android:layout_gravity="center"
        tools:layout="@layout/fragment_main"/>
</FrameLayout>
```

This defines a FrameLayout view that covers the whole screen, with a fragment of class MainFragment floating inside of it. If you like your code all lined up properly, select the Code > Reformat Code menu option or use the keyboard shortcut (Ctrl+Alt+L on Windows).

(If you're typing this into Android Studio, you'll notice that some of the text is displayed in red, and there's an error shown in the preview window if it's open. That happens because we haven't defined those two missing parts yet. They'll be added shortly.)

FrameLayout is one of several Layout views supported by Android. These views arrange other views inside of them to create a desired effect. Many types of layouts are available, and you can create your own. Here's a summary of the most common types you're likely to need in your programs:

FrameLayout

   Shows one or more child views on top of each other.

GridLayout

   Arranges its child views into rows and columns.

LinearLayout

   Displays its children in a single column or row.

RelativeLayout

   A flexible layout that arranges views in relation to other views.

For a complete list of Android layouts and details about the options you can set on each one, see the online documentation.[4]

Since we only have one child view, it doesn't really matter which one we use in terms of how it will look. FrameLayout is the simplest and most efficient, so we should use that one.

Attributes of the FrameLayout tag

Every XML tag has attributes that control what it does. Let's look at the attributes that we set on the FrameLayout tag more closely:

xmlns:android="http://schemas.android.com/apk/res/android"
> Defines the android namespace,[5] so that android: will be accepted in subsequent attribute names.

xmlns:tools="http://schemas.android.com/tools"
> Defines the tools namespace.

android:layout_width="match_parent"
> Sets the width of the view to cover the entire width of the parent. Since this is the top-level element, that means it will cover the screen. Possible values are match_parent, wrap_content, or an absolute width value.

android:layout_height="match_parent"
> Sets the height of the view to cover the height of the parent (screen). Every view has to have a width and height.

tools:context=".TicTacToeActivity"
> Indicates that this layout file is used by the TicTacToeActivity class. Unlike the other attributes, this one is just for the visual editor and isn't used at runtime.

Attributes of the fragment Tag

Here's the meaning of all the attributes we used on the fragment tag:

android:id="@+id/fragment_main"
> Defines a new resource identifier called fragment_main that can be used in code or other XML attributes. "@+" means we're defining something new, whereas "@" means we're referring to something already defined elsewhere.

---

4. http://d.android.com/guide/topics/ui/declaring-layout.html
5. http://en.wikipedia.org/wiki/XML_namespace

class="org.example.tictactoe.MainFragment"

Lets Android know that this fragment is an instance of the MainFragment class. In other words, when Android goes to create this object from the XML, it will actually create a MainFragment. This class will be defined in *Defining a Fragment in the Main Activity*, on page 41.

android:layout_width="wrap_content"

Sets the width of the fragment to be defined by the width of its content.

android:layout_height="wrap_content"

Sets the height of the fragment to the height of its content.

android:layout_gravity="center"

Centers this fragment inside its parent. Possible values include top, bottom, left, right, top, bottom, center, and fill, among others. Gravity values can be combined using a vertical bar—for example, top|right.

tools:layout="@layout/fragment_main"

Refers to another XML file that defines the contents of this fragment.

Creating the Main Fragment

The main fragment contains the buttons to continue the game, start a new game, and display information about the game. We define that in fragment_main.xml.

Create the file by clicking on the activity_main.xml file, pressing Ctrl+C (Copy), and then pressing Ctrl+V (Paste). When it prompts for a new name, enter fragment_main.xml. (There are other ways to do this, such as using a wizard, but this is the fastest way for me.)

Replace the contents of fragment_main.xml with the following text:

```
ticTacToev1/src/main/res/layout/fragment_main.xml
<LinearLayout
    xmlns:android="http://schemas.android.com/apk/res/android"
    xmlns:tools="http://schemas.android.com/tools"
    android:layout_width="wrap_content"
    android:layout_height="wrap_content"
    android:background="@drawable/menu_background"
    android:elevation="@dimen/elevation_high"
    android:orientation="vertical"
    android:padding="@dimen/menu_padding"
    tools:context=".TicTacToeActivity">

    <TextView
        android:layout_width="wrap_content"
        android:layout_height="wrap_content"
```

```
        android:layout_marginBottom="@dimen/menu_space"
        android:text="@string/long_app_name"
        android:textAppearance="?android:textAppearanceLarge"
        android:textSize="@dimen/menu_text_size"/>

    <Button
        android:id="@+id/continue_button"
        android:layout_width="match_parent"
        android:layout_height="wrap_content"
        android:layout_margin="@dimen/menu_button_margin"
        android:padding="@dimen/menu_button_padding"
        android:text="@string/continue_label"/>

    <Button
        android:id="@+id/new_button"
        android:layout_width="match_parent"
        android:layout_height="wrap_content"
        android:layout_gravity="center"
        android:layout_margin="@dimen/menu_button_margin"
        android:padding="@dimen/menu_button_padding"
        android:text="@string/new_game_label"/>

    <Button
        android:id="@+id/about_button"
        android:layout_width="match_parent"
        android:layout_height="wrap_content"
        android:layout_gravity="center"
        android:layout_margin="@dimen/menu_button_margin"
        android:padding="@dimen/menu_button_padding"
        android:text="@string/about_label"/>
</LinearLayout>
```

Lots of red lines will appear. Don't worry—we'll fix all those by the end of the chapter.

In this example we want a column with four items so we use a LinearLayout with android:orientation="vertical". Inside the linear layout we define a text view and three buttons.

Text views are probably the most common type of user interface element that you'll encounter in Android development. Here are a few more:

Button
    A push-button control.

CheckBox
    A two-state button for a multiple choice list.

EditText
    An editable text view.

ImageButton

> A button that displays an image instead of text.

ListView

> Shows items in a vertically scrolling list.

RadioButton

> A single selection two-state button.

VideoView

> Displays a video file.

WebView

> Displays web pages.

For a full list, see the documentation of the View class.[6]

Attributes of the LinearLayout Tag

Here are the new attributes on the LinearLayout tag:

android:background="@drawable/menu_background"

> Sets a background drawable for the entire view. A drawable can be a color, image, or compound object defined in another XML file. More on that in a moment.

android:elevation="@dimen/elevation_high"

> Raises the view off the canvas by a small amount. This causes a shadow to be drawn under the view in Android 5.0 (Lollipop) and later. Like all unrecognized attributes, it will be ignored if you run the program on older versions. Instead of specifying the amount with a number, we refer to a dimension that will be defined in another XML file.

android:orientation="vertical"

> Specifies direction of the layout. Possible values are vertical, which arranges the children in a column, and horizontal, which arranges them in a row. If you need both horizontal and vertical, you'll have to use a different layout such as GridLayout.

android:padding="@dimen/menu_padding"

> Tells Android to leave a little space all around the inside of the view. If you need the space to be outside the view, use margin instead.

Indirect values such as "@dimen/menu_padding" are extremely powerful, but can be a little confusing at times. Android Studio helps by showing the final

---

6.   http://d.android.com/reference/android/view/View.html

resolved value in the editor if possible. Once it's defined, you can hover your mouse or click on the value to see the original reference, and Ctrl+click on the reference to go to its definition.

Attributes of the TextView Tag

We use the following attributes on the TextView tag:

android:layout_marginBottom="@dimen/menu_space"
> This is used on the text view to leave a gap between the text and the buttons.

android:text="@string/long_app_name"
> Specifies the text to display. In this case it's a reference to the long_app_name value defined in the strings file.

android:textAppearance="?android:textAppearanceLarge"
> Makes the text larger and bolder than usual. The "?" means this is a reference to a constant defined in the current theme. A theme defines hundreds of constants to control the appearance and behavior of every view in the app. See *Styles and Themes*, on page 46 for more info.

android:textSize="@dimen/menu_text_size"
> Even with the textAppearance attribute, the text looked like it needed to be a little larger, so we hard-coded a bigger size here.

Attributes of the Button Tag

The Button tag uses these attributes:

android:layout_margin="@dimen/menu_button_margin"
> Allows for some extra space around the outside of the button.

android:padding="@dimen/menu_button_padding"
> Specifies some extra space *inside* the button as well.

android:text="@string/continue_label"
> Displays text on the button. This is another reference to the strings file.

We'll define all those "@" values in *Defining Resources*, on page 43. First, let's work on the Java code that goes with the XML.

Filling In the Code

Now that we have the layouts of the main screen and fragment, we need to write a little Java code to make them appear. We'll start with the app's main program: the MainActivity class.

Defining the Main Activity

You should already have a file called MainActivity.java in the org.example.tictactoe package under the java folder. It was created by Android Studio when we created the project. Open it now by double-clicking it in the Project window, by selecting the Navigate > File menu option, or by pressing the keyboard shortcut (Ctrl+Shift+N on Windows) and typing the filename. Then replace all the code with the following:

ticTacToev1/src/main/java/org/example/tictactoe/MainActivity.java

```
Line 1   package org.example.tictactoe;
    -
    -    import android.app.Activity;
    -    import android.os.Bundle;
    5
    -    public class MainActivity extends Activity {
    -
    -        @Override
    -        protected void onCreate(Bundle savedInstanceState) {
   10            super.onCreate(savedInstanceState);
    -            setContentView(R.layout.activity_main);
    -        }
    -    }
```

Since this is the first Java code we've seen so far, let's go over each line and describe what it does.

Line 1 defines the package name. Java source files are gathered into packages for easier access and to prevent name collisions. The package name should always match the directory name.

Lines 3 and 4 tell the compiler we're going to use the Activity class from the android.app package and the Bundle class from the android.os package. These are standard packages provided by the Android framework.

On line 6, we begin the definition of a class called MainActivity, which is a subclass of the Activity class. Activities are discussed in *Activities*, on page 19.

Line 9 starts the onCreate() method, which is called as part of the activity life cycle when the activity is first created. @Override is a hint that this method was originally defined in the Activity class, but we're going to provide a new definition for it. The first thing we do in the new definition is call the old definition on line 10.

Line 11 is the important part. It fills in the activity's contents with the XML layout defined in activity_main.xml. This is how the XML we declared earlier is used.

Finally, the last couple of lines close the brace blocks opened earlier. Everything must be properly nested or you'll get errors from the compiler.

Next, we'll define the fragment used in the main activity.

Defining a Fragment in the Main Activity

In *Creating the Main Screen*, on page 33 we created a fragment with a class named org.example.tictactoe.MainFragment. Let's define that class now.

Create MainFragment.java by finding MainActivity.java and duplicating it. Give the duplicate the name MainFragment.java, and then when it opens, replace the code with the following:

ticTacToev1/src/main/java/org/example/tictactoe/MainFragment.java
```
package org.example.tictactoe;

import android.app.AlertDialog;
import android.app.Fragment;
import android.content.DialogInterface;
import android.os.Bundle;
import android.view.LayoutInflater;
import android.view.View;
import android.view.ViewGroup;

public class MainFragment extends Fragment {

    private AlertDialog mDialog;

    @Override
    public View onCreateView(LayoutInflater inflater, ViewGroup container,
                             Bundle savedInstanceState) {
        View rootView = inflater.inflate(R.layout.fragment_main, container, false);
        // Handle buttons here...
        return rootView;
    }
}
```

The structure of this class is similar to the MainActivity class, except that the starting method of a fragment is onCreateView(). It takes three parameters: an inflater object that we can use to turn XML into a view, a reference to the parent container, and some saved state. We don't need the saved state, but we call the inflater.inflate() method on R.layout.fragment_main (a reference to fragment_main.xml defined earlier) and return the view it created.

Inside the main fragment are three buttons for continuing a game in progress, starting a game, and reading about the game. Let's implement the easiest one first.

Adding an About Box

Many apps have a button where you can get more information or help on the program. You may want to display credits about all the people who helped with the program, open source packages you used, or other legal information. For this example, we want to display a couple of paragraphs about how to play the game when the user presses the About button. The following screenshot shows what it will look like:

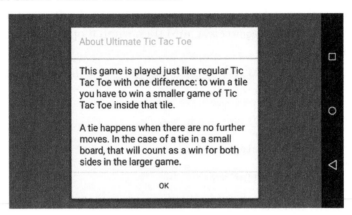

To implement this, we need to add a few lines to the fragment's onCreateView() method. Before returning the rootView, add this code:

ticTacToev1/src/main/java/org/example/tictactoe/MainFragment.java

```
Line 1  // Handle buttons here...
   -    View aboutButton = rootView.findViewById(R.id.about_button);
   -    aboutButton.setOnClickListener(new View.OnClickListener() {
   -        @Override
   5        public void onClick(View view) {
   -            AlertDialog.Builder builder =
   -                    new AlertDialog.Builder(getActivity());
   -            builder.setTitle(R.string.about_title);
   -            builder.setMessage(R.string.about_text);
  10            builder.setCancelable(false);
   -            builder.setPositiveButton(R.string.ok_label,
   -                    new DialogInterface.OnClickListener() {
   -                        @Override
   -                        public void onClick(DialogInterface dialogInterface,
  15                                            int i) {
   -                            // nothing
   -                        }
   -                    });
   -            mDialog = builder.show();
  20        }
   -    });
```

This searches the fragment view for the About button on line 2, and then sets a click listener on it on line 3. The listener's onClick() method (line 5) will be called when the user taps on the button.

On line 6, we create a new instance of AlertDialog.Builder, passing it the current activity. Then starting on line 8 we set the title and message contents of the dialog. The setCancelable() call on line 10 tells Android not to dismiss the dialog when the user taps outside the box. The dialog has one OK button, defined on line 11, which does nothing.

Once the dialog is defined, we then show it on line 19.

There's one more thing we need. When the activity containing the fragment is paused—for example, if another app is started—we want the About box to go away. To do this, add this onPause() method inside the MainFragment class:

ticTacToev1/src/main/java/org/example/tictactoe/MainFragment.java
```
@Override
public void onPause() {
   super.onPause();

   // Get rid of the about dialog if it's still up
   if (mDialog != null)
      mDialog.dismiss();
}
```

There should now be two methods nested in MainFragment: onCreateView() and onPause(). If you get any compiler errors, check that all the curly braces match up. Pull the completed source file down from the website[7] if you're still having trouble.

Defining Resources

Almost all resources are defined with XML (see *Using Resources*, on page 21). Thankfully, the XML is precompiled at build time so you don't have to pay a performance penalty for parsing it when the program runs.

Strings

Instead of hard-coding text strings in our program code and layouts, we store them all in one place: the strings.xml resource file in the res/values folder. That will make it much easier to translate the strings when it comes time to internationalize your app for foreign markets. Here are the definitions for all the strings we've used so far in the Tic-Tac-Toe program:

---

7.   http://pragprog.com/book/eband4

ticTacToev1/src/main/res/values/strings.xml

```xml
<?xml version="1.0" encoding="utf-8"?>
<resources>
    <string name="app_name">UT3</string>
    <string name="long_app_name">Ultimate Tic Tac Toe</string>
    <string name="action_settings">Settings</string>
    <string name="continue_label">Continue</string>
    <string name="new_game_label">New Game</string>
    <string name="about_label">About</string>
    <string name="ok_label">OK</string>
    <string name="about_title">About Ultimate Tic Tac Toe</string>
    <string name="about_text">\
This game is played just like regular Tic Tac Toe with one difference: to
win a tile you have to win a smaller game of Tic Tac Toe inside that tile.\n\
\n\
A tie happens when there are no further moves. In the case of a tie in a small
board, that will count as a win for both sides in the larger game.
</string>
</resources>
```

Each resource has a name and a value. The name is used in Java code or in XML to refer to the resource id. For example, in Java, R.string.app_name would be the id number of the app_name resource. To get the actual string you'd have to call another function such as Activity.getString(), and pass it that id. In XML it's a little simpler: you just say "@" followed by the resource type and name—for example, @string/app_name.

We'll look at how to specify alternate resources in *Specifying Alternate Resources*, on page 120.

Dimensions

Dimension resources can be used anywhere a length is used. Putting them together in a dimensions file (dimens.xml in the res/values folder) helps you support different sizes of Android devices without having to change the code. So far, our app is using the following dimensions:

ticTacToev1/src/main/res/values/dimens.xml

```xml
<resources>
    <dimen name="elevation_high">8dp</dimen>
    <dimen name="stroke_width">1dp</dimen>
    <dimen name="corner_radius">4dp</dimen>
    <dimen name="menu_padding">10dp</dimen>
    <dimen name="menu_space">10dp</dimen>
    <dimen name="menu_text_size">32sp</dimen>
    <dimen name="menu_button_margin">4dp</dimen>
    <dimen name="menu_button_padding">10dp</dimen>
</resources>
```

See *Dps vs. Sps*, on page 47 for an explanation of what "dp" and "sp" mean.

You may see two versions of the dimens.xml file: a regular one and one marked w820dp. Just use the regular one for now. The other one is an alternate resource for wide screens. We'll study alternate resources in *Specifying Alternate Resources*, on page 120.

Drawables

Drawables are any kind of graphical objects that can be drawn on the screen. The simplest drawables are bitmaps, which are typically stored in PNG or JPG format. An example of a bitmap is the launcher icon displayed on the home screen for your app.

Drawables can also be created in XML. Here's the definition of the background drawable used for the options on the main screen. Put it in the res/drawable folder:

ticTacToev1/src/main/res/drawable/menu_background.xml
```xml
<?xml version="1.0" encoding="utf-8"?>
<shape
    xmlns:android="http://schemas.android.com/apk/res/android"
    android:shape="rectangle">
    <stroke
        android:width="@dimen/stroke_width"
        android:color="@color/border_color"/>
    <solid android:color="@color/field_color"/>
    <corners android:radius="@dimen/corner_radius"/>
</shape>
```

It defines a rectangle shape with rounded corners and a solid interior. Note how it refers to other resources for the width and radius of the outline and all the colors.

You could do this with a bitmap, but XML has the advantage of being vector based with infinite resolution. That means no matter how big you need this background to be blown up, it will always be sharp and not pixelated.

Here are the most common types of drawables:

Bitmap file
> A picture in PNG, JPG, or GIF format. PNG bitmaps can be partially transparent.

Nine-patch file
> A PNG with stretchable regions to allow resizing based on content.

Layer list

> An array of other drawables, drawn in order.

State list

> A list of alternatives for different states.

Level list

> A list of alternatives for different level values.

Shape

> A geometric figure including lines and colors.

See the online documentation[8] for a complete list of drawable types and attributes.

Colors

Here's the definition for the colors used in the background resource earlier:

ticTacToev1/src/main/res/values/colors.xml

```
<?xml version="1.0" encoding="utf-8"?>
<resources>
    <color name="field_color">#b5cee0</color>
    <color name="border_color">#7f7f7f</color>
</resources>
```

Colors in Android are specified in the form "#RRGGBB" or "#AARRGGBB" where "RR," "GG," and "BB" are the red, green, and blue components in hexadecimal, and "AA" is the alpha component. Hex numbers range from "00" (0) to "FF" (255). For example, "#FF0000" is pure red, whereas "#FFFFFF" is white.

The optional alpha component specifies how transparent the color will be, from 0 (fully transparent) to 255 (fully opaque). If you leave off the alpha, then the color will be opaque.

Styles and Themes

Styles and themes play an important role in how your app looks. A *theme* is a collection of styles, and a *style* is a set of values that control appearances and behaviors. If you open up the AndroidManifest.xml file you'll see this line:

```
android:theme="@style/AppTheme"
```

This refers to the theme AppTheme defined in styles.xml. Ctrl+click on AppTheme to open the file and change it to the following:

---

8. http://d.android.com/guide/topics/resources/drawable-resource.html

ticTacToev1/src/main/res/values/styles.xml

```
<?xml version="1.0" encoding="utf-8"?>
<resources>
    <!-- Base application theme. -->
    <style name="AppTheme"
           parent="android:Theme.Holo.Light.NoActionBar.Fullscreen">
        <!-- Customize your theme here. -->
    </style>
</resources>
```

Themes define hundreds of values, so typically you want to just use one that is already defined plus a few changes. You do that with the parent= attribute. In this case we're using a theme that has no title bar across the top that takes up the entire screen.

You can see all the available themes in the Android Studio editor by placing your cursor after android:Theme. and pressing Ctrl+Space. After we get the app running, you might want to come back and play around with different themes to see how they affect it.

Dps vs. Sps

Historically, programmers always designed computer interfaces in terms of pixels. For example, you might make a field 300 pixels wide, allow 5 pixels of spacing between columns, and define icons 16-by-16 pixels in size. The problem is that if you run that program on new displays with more and more dots per inch (dpi), the user interface appears smaller and smaller. At some point, it becomes too hard to read.

Resolution-independent measurements help solve this problem. Android supports all the following units:

- px (pixels): Dots on the screen.

- in (inches): Size as measured by a ruler.

- mm (millimeters): Size as measured by a ruler.

- pt (points): 1/72 of an inch.

- dp (density-independent pixels): An abstract unit based on the density of the screen. On a display with 160 dots per inch, 1dp = 1px.

- dip: Synonym for dp.

- sp (scale-independent pixels): Similar to dp but also scaled by the user's font size preference.

To make your interface scalable to any current and future type of display, I recommend you always use the sp unit for text sizes and the dp unit for everything else. Avoid using pixels (px) for anything.

Running the Game

All the pieces are in place for the game to work now. Give it a try by selecting Run > Run 'app', by clicking the Run button on the toolbar, or pressing the keyboard shortcut (Shift+F10 on Windows). Just like with the Hello, Android program, you're prompted to choose a device. Pick either an emulator or a physical device hooked up through USB.

If all goes well, you'll see a screen like our original figure on page 33. If you press the Continue or the New Game button, nothing will happen (those will be added in the next chapter). If you select the About button, the About dialog box should pop up. Press OK to dismiss it.

Joe asks:

How Do You Get Out?

You may have noticed there's no exit button in the game. That's because it's not needed, and having one goes against the Android design guidelines.[a] To exit the game, simply press the Back or Home button, or select the Recent Apps button and pick some other app on the list.

If you're worried about leaving the program running, don't be. Android will take care of removing the program and its resources when they're needed by other programs. To force a program to go away, press the Recent Apps button and swipe the program away. This not only removes it from the list, but it also kills the app and recovers its resources. This is sometimes useful in development and with a few buggy programs, but in the vast majority of cases it's completely unnecessary.

a.   http://d.android.com/design

Debugging

If you've been programming for any length of time, you know that some (most?) of the time, things don't go the way you expect. What do you do then? Luckily, the same techniques you use to diagnose problems on other platforms can be applied to Android. These include printing messages to the log and stepping through your program in a debugger.

Debugging with Log Messages

The class provides several static methods to print messages of various severity levels to the Android system log:

- Log.e(): Errors
- Log.w(): Warnings
- Log.i(): Information
- Log.d(): Debugging
- Log.v(): Verbose
- Log.wtf(): What a Terrible Failure

Users will never see the system log, but as a developer you can view it in a couple of ways. In Android Studio, the LogCat view is shown at the bottom of the window when the program is running (see the following figure). You can reduce the number of lines shown by specifying a log level other than Verbose, or by typing a string into the filter field.

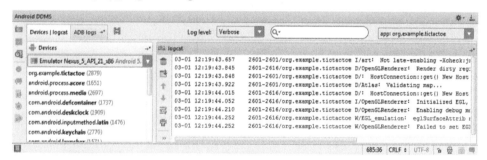

Simply add lines to the program such as

```
Log.d("UT3", "Got to point A");
```

and next time you run the program they'll show up in the log.

If you're not using Android Studio, you can see the same output by running the adb logcat command[9] from the SDK's platform-tools directory. You may want to start this command in a separate window and leave it running whenever the emulator is running or the device is connected. It won't interfere with any other monitors.

I can't stress enough how useful the Android log will be during development. Any time you get an unexpected error, look in the log first. Nine times out of ten, it will have enough information to diagnose the problem without having to bring out the heavy guns: the debugger.

---

9.   http://d.android.com/tools/help/adb.html

Debugging with the Debugger

The ultimate way to diagnose a problem with your Android program is the debugger in Android Studio. To start the debugger, select Run > Debug instead of Run > Run. Or you can click the debug button in the icon bar, or use the keyboard shortcut (Shift+F9 on Windows).

When running under the debugger, the app will stop whenever an exception occurs or it reaches a breakpoint. A breakpoint is like a stop sign that you put in your code. In the Java editor, click the gutter to the left of the line where you want to stop. A red icon appears, and the next time the program gets to that line it will pause execution.

Once stopped, a debug window will appear at the bottom of the screen, as shown in the following figure. It displays your current location and the values of all your variables.

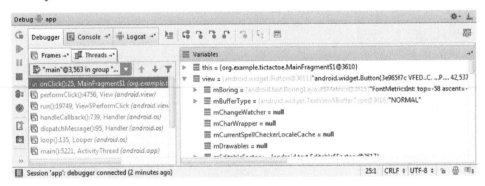

From there you can examine variables and class members, see the sequence of calls that got you to this point (the traceback), continue until the next breakpoint, or single step through the program one line at a time.

Testing

In addition to ad hoc testing (that is, just trying things to see if they work), I highly recommend you use automated tests whenever possible. You could run many different kinds of tests, but here are the most common types:

Unit tests[10]

Check the low-level functionality of your program. They're based on the JUnit framework[11] and are supported by Android Studio and gradle.

---

10. http://d.android.com/tools/testing/testing_android.html

11. http://junit.org

User interface tests[12]

> Verify that your user interface is functional. Generally they do so by driving your user interface through a series of interactions via a scripting language.

Monkey tests[13]

> Try to break your program by bombarding it with random input. Imagine thousands of monkeys lined up in a room, pressing random buttons on the screen until something crashes.

Although it's not trivial to set up, automated testing is essential for professional projects. A full treatment of automated testing is beyond the scope of this book, but a number of tutorials and guides are available online.

Fast-Forward >>

Whew, that was a lot to cover in one chapter! Starting from scratch, you used layout files to organize your user interface and Android resources for text, colors, and more. You created Java classes for an activity and a fragment, and you added controls such as buttons and text fields.

Android is a complex system, but you don't have to know all of it to get started. When you need help, the hundreds of pages of reference material online go into more depth on all the classes and methods used here.

To view the online documentation, open the docs subdirectory of your Android SDK install directory, or point your browser to http://d.android.com. And of course, if you get stuck, you can always drop by the discussion forum for this book.[14] The other readers and I will be happy to help you out. Another good resource is Stack Overflow,[15] or just use Google.

(Believe it or not, it was possible to program before Google and the web. But nowadays when the network is down, it's downright hard to get anything done. That's another good reason to own lots of books!)

---

12. http://d.android.com/tools/testing/testing_ui.html
13. http://d.android.com/tools/help/monkey.html
14. https://forums.pragprog.com/forums/231
15. http://stackoverflow.com/questions/tagged/android

CHAPTER 4

Defining the Game Interface

In the previous chapter we created a game called Ultimate Tic-Tac-Toe and implemented an opening screen for it. What did we leave out? Oh yes, the game part. We'll tackle that in two chapters. In this chapter, we'll work on the user interface for the game. You'll be able to play it with another person by passing your phone or tablet back and forth. In the next chapter we'll give the game the ability to think and make its own moves, so you can play it by yourself.

The Game Board

We'll build up the game board by starting from the smallest part and moving to larger and larger parts as we go. Depending on how your brain works, you could start with the top-level objects and move downward. It's up to you, but this way works best for me.

Starting Small

First, take a look back at Figure 2, *Tic-Tac-Toe meets Inception*, on page 32 and think about what it will take to implement that. What comes to mind first? Probably the X and O symbols, so let's do them first.

You can make up your own, or download mine from the book's website[1] (they're part of the ticTacToev2 example code). I created x_blue.png and o_red.png using a free editor called Inkscape,[2] and saved them as fairly large, 128×128px PNG files. PNG files can have transparent or translucent backgrounds so they can be overlaid on top of other graphics.

These were saved in the drawable-xxhdpi directory, where the "xxhdpi" suffix stands for "extra extra high" density, or around 400 dots per inch. Android devices can also have medium, high, and extra high density screens, and Android will automatically scale the images up or down if necessary. You can create a different set of bitmaps for each screen density, but for this it was overkill. (See *Specifying Alternate Resources*, on page 120 for more information about using suffixes on resource directories.)

To create a directory in Android Studio, right-click on the parent directory (res in this case) and select New > Directory, and then enter the directory name. You could also use the Android resource directory wizard, but I find that the simplest way is the best. The drawable-xxhdpi directory won't appear when you're using the default Android mode on the Project window, but it's there. If you try to paste into the drawable folder, you'll be prompted for the destination directory.

I don't think we have enough XML yet, so let's wrap these in a drawable called tile.xml. Remember, XML drawables go in the drawable directory. Here's the definition:

```
ticTacToev2/src/main/res/drawable/tile.xml
<?xml version="1.0" encoding="utf-8"?>
<level-list xmlns:android="http://schemas.android.com/apk/res/android" >
    <item
        android:drawable="@drawable/x_blue"
        android:maxLevel="0" />
    <item
        android:drawable="@drawable/o_red"
        android:maxLevel="1" />
    <item
        android:drawable="@drawable/tile_empty"
        android:maxLevel="2" />
    <item
        android:drawable="@drawable/tile_available"
        android:maxLevel="3" />
</level-list>
```

1. http://pragprog.com/book/eband4
2. http://www.inkscape.org

A tile has four levels: X, O, Empty, and Available. X and O are pretty easy—they refer to the x_blue and o_red bitmaps we just created. Here's the definition of the empty tile:

ticTacToev2/src/main/res/drawable/tile_empty.xml
```xml
<?xml version="1.0" encoding="utf-8"?>
<shape xmlns:android="http://schemas.android.com/apk/res/android"
       android:shape="rectangle">
  <stroke
      android:width="@dimen/stroke_width"
      android:color="@color/dark_border_color"/>
    <corners android:radius="@dimen/corner_radius"/>
</shape>
```

It defines a rounded rectangle with a dark border. The available tile is similar, just with a green color (specified by reference) in the middle:

ticTacToev2/src/main/res/drawable/tile_available.xml
```xml
<?xml version="1.0" encoding="utf-8"?>
<shape xmlns:android="http://schemas.android.com/apk/res/android"
       android:shape="rectangle">
  <stroke
      android:width="@dimen/stroke_width"
      android:color="@color/dark_border_color"/>
    <solid android:color="@color/available_color"/>
    <corners android:radius="@dimen/corner_radius"/>
</shape>
```

We'll use a tile.xml for all eighty-one small tiles on the screen and set the level so that it will take on one of its four possible appearances in each instance.

Chairman of the Board

A small board is just nine tiles arranged in a 3x3 grid. We specify a row and column number to make each tile appear in the right place. Note that the indices start at 0.

ticTacToev2/src/main/res/layout/small_board.xml
```xml
<GridLayout
  xmlns:android="http://schemas.android.com/apk/res/android"
  xmlns:tools="http://schemas.android.com/tools"
  android:layout_width="wrap_content"
  android:layout_height="wrap_content"
  android:background="@drawable/tile_background"
  android:elevation="@dimen/elevation_low"
  android:padding="@dimen/small_board_padding"
  tools:context=".GameActivity">

  <ImageButton android:id="@+id/small1" style="@style/TileButton"
               android:layout_column="0" android:layout_row="0"/>
```

```
<ImageButton android:id="@+id/small2" style="@style/TileButton"
                 android:layout_column="1" android:layout_row="0"/>
<ImageButton android:id="@+id/small3" style="@style/TileButton"
                 android:layout_column="2" android:layout_row="0"/>
<ImageButton android:id="@+id/small4" style="@style/TileButton"
                 android:layout_column="0" android:layout_row="1"/>
<ImageButton android:id="@+id/small5" style="@style/TileButton"
                 android:layout_column="1" android:layout_row="1"/>
<ImageButton android:id="@+id/small6" style="@style/TileButton"
                 android:layout_column="2" android:layout_row="1"/>
<ImageButton android:id="@+id/small7" style="@style/TileButton"
                 android:layout_column="0" android:layout_row="2"/>
<ImageButton android:id="@+id/small8" style="@style/TileButton"
                 android:layout_column="1" android:layout_row="2"/>
<ImageButton android:id="@+id/small9" style="@style/TileButton"
                 android:layout_column="2" android:layout_row="2"/>
</GridLayout>
```

Each tile is an ImageButton, which as you might have guessed is a cross between an Image and a Button. It's an image you can press, since we'll need to press the buttons to make our moves.

Each button specifies its row and column number, and a style called TileButton. To define this style, open the styles.xml file and add this before the closing </resources> tag:

ticTacToev2/src/main/res/values/styles.xml

```
<style name="TileButton">
    <item name="android:layout_width">@dimen/tile_size</item>
    <item name="android:layout_height">@dimen/tile_size</item>
    <item name="android:layout_margin">@dimen/tile_margin</item>
    <item name="android:background">#00000000</item>
    <item name="android:padding">@dimen/tile_padding</item>
    <item name="android:scaleType">centerCrop</item>
    <item name="android:src">@drawable/tile</item>
</style>
```

Why did we have to use a style here? OK, I admit it, we didn't. I just got tired of repeating the same values over and over again. It's not laziness; it's the DRY (Don't Repeat Yourself) principle. For more information on the DRY principle and other great tips on the art of programming, see *The Pragmatic Programmer [HT99]*.

Background Information

In the small tile definition, you may have noticed this line:

```
android:background="@drawable/tile_background"
```

What's that about? Well, if you look back at the screenshot (Figure 2, *Tic-Tac-Toe meets Inception*, on page 32) you'll see that each small board can have a state, just like each tile.

Here's the definition for tile_background.xml:

```
ticTacToev2/src/main/res/drawable/tile_background.xml
<?xml version="1.0" encoding="utf-8"?>
<level-list xmlns:android="http://schemas.android.com/apk/res/android">
    <item
        android:drawable="@drawable/tile_blue"
        android:maxLevel="0"/>
    <item
        android:drawable="@drawable/tile_red"
        android:maxLevel="1"/>
    <item
        android:drawable="@drawable/tile_gray"
        android:maxLevel="2"/>
    <item
        android:drawable="@drawable/tile_purple"
        android:maxLevel="3"/>
</level-list>
```

We use a blue color if X owns the board, red if O owns the board, gray if nobody owns it, and purple if both players own it (that is, the small board is tied). The definitions of those drawables are pretty straightforward. I'll include them here for completeness.

Here's the definition of the blue tile, used for small boards owned by the X player:

```
ticTacToev2/src/main/res/drawable/tile_blue.xml
<?xml version="1.0" encoding="utf-8"?>
<shape xmlns:android="http://schemas.android.com/apk/res/android"
        android:shape="rectangle">
    <stroke
        android:width="@dimen/stroke_width"
        android:color="@color/dark_border_color"/>
    <solid android:color="@color/blue_color"/>
    <corners android:radius="@dimen/corner_radius"/>
</shape>
```

A red tile is used for boards owned by O:

```
ticTacToev2/src/main/res/drawable/tile_red.xml
<?xml version="1.0" encoding="utf-8"?>
<shape xmlns:android="http://schemas.android.com/apk/res/android"
        android:shape="rectangle">
    <stroke
        android:width="@dimen/stroke_width"
        android:color="@color/dark_border_color"/>
```

```
    <solid android:color="@color/red_color"/>
    <corners android:radius="@dimen/corner_radius"/>
</shape>
```

Gray tiles aren't owned by any player:

ticTacToev2/src/main/res/drawable/tile_gray.xml

```
<?xml version="1.0" encoding="utf-8"?>
<shape xmlns:android="http://schemas.android.com/apk/res/android"
       android:shape="rectangle">
    <stroke
        android:width="@dimen/stroke_width"
        android:color="@color/dark_border_color"/>
    <solid android:color="@color/gray_color"/>
    <corners android:radius="@dimen/corner_radius"/>
</shape>
```

Purple tiles are owned by both players:

ticTacToev2/src/main/res/drawable/tile_purple.xml

```
<?xml version="1.0" encoding="utf-8"?>
<shape xmlns:android="http://schemas.android.com/apk/res/android"
       android:shape="rectangle">
    <stroke
        android:width="@dimen/stroke_width"
        android:color="@color/dark_border_color"/>
    <solid android:color="@color/purple_color"/>
    <corners android:radius="@dimen/corner_radius"/>
</shape>
```

All the tiles consist of a 1dp rounded rectangle filled with the appropriate color.

Large and in Charge

Now let's define the large board. No surprises here: it's a 3×3 grid of small boards:

ticTacToev2/src/main/res/layout/large_board.xml

```
<GridLayout
    xmlns:android="http://schemas.android.com/apk/res/android"
    xmlns:tools="http://schemas.android.com/tools"
    android:layout_width="wrap_content"
    android:layout_height="wrap_content"
    tools:context=".GameActivity">

    <include android:id="@+id/large1" layout="@layout/small_board"
        android:layout_width="wrap_content" android:layout_height="wrap_content"
        android:layout_margin="@dimen/small_board_margin"
        android:layout_column="0" android:layout_row="0"/>
    <include android:id="@+id/large2" layout="@layout/small_board"
```

```
        android:layout_width="wrap_content" android:layout_height="wrap_content"
        android:layout_margin="@dimen/small_board_margin"
        android:layout_column="1" android:layout_row="0"/>
    <include android:id="@+id/large3" layout="@layout/small_board"
        android:layout_width="wrap_content" android:layout_height="wrap_content"
        android:layout_margin="@dimen/small_board_margin"
        android:layout_column="2" android:layout_row="0"/>
    <include android:id="@+id/large4" layout="@layout/small_board"
        android:layout_width="wrap_content" android:layout_height="wrap_content"
        android:layout_margin="@dimen/small_board_margin"
        android:layout_column="0" android:layout_row="1"/>
    <include android:id="@+id/large5" layout="@layout/small_board"
        android:layout_width="wrap_content" android:layout_height="wrap_content"
        android:layout_margin="@dimen/small_board_margin"
        android:layout_column="1" android:layout_row="1"/>
    <include android:id="@+id/large6" layout="@layout/small_board"
        android:layout_width="wrap_content" android:layout_height="wrap_content"
        android:layout_margin="@dimen/small_board_margin"
        android:layout_column="2" android:layout_row="1"/>
    <include android:id="@+id/large7" layout="@layout/small_board"
        android:layout_width="wrap_content" android:layout_height="wrap_content"
        android:layout_margin="@dimen/small_board_margin"
        android:layout_column="0" android:layout_row="2"/>
    <include android:id="@+id/large8" layout="@layout/small_board"
        android:layout_width="wrap_content" android:layout_height="wrap_content"
        android:layout_margin="@dimen/small_board_margin"
        android:layout_column="1" android:layout_row="2"/>
    <include android:id="@+id/large9" layout="@layout/small_board"
        android:layout_width="wrap_content" android:layout_height="wrap_content"
        android:layout_margin="@dimen/small_board_margin"
        android:layout_column="2" android:layout_row="2"/>
</GridLayout>
```

Hmm, that <include> tag is new. It creates an instance of the layout specified
by the layout= attribute, merges in the values of the other attributes, and then
places the view at that spot in the parent layout. We could've just copied and
pasted small_board.xml in there nine times, but we're lazy. I mean DRY.

Putting It All Together

Now that we have the definition of the large board, let's wrap a fragment
around it:

ticTacToev2/src/main/res/layout/fragment_game.xml
```
<RelativeLayout
    xmlns:android="http://schemas.android.com/apk/res/android"
    xmlns:tools="http://schemas.android.com/tools"
    android:layout_width="wrap_content"
    android:layout_height="wrap_content"
    tools:context=".GameActivity">
```

```
<include
    layout="@layout/large_board"
    android:layout_width="wrap_content"
    android:layout_height="wrap_content"/>

</RelativeLayout>
```

and stick that fragment into an activity along with a background image:

ticTacToev2/src/main/res/layout/activity_game.xml

```
<FrameLayout
    xmlns:android="http://schemas.android.com/apk/res/android"
    xmlns:tools="http://schemas.android.com/tools"
    android:layout_width="match_parent"
    android:layout_height="match_parent"
    tools:context=".TicTacToeActivity">

    <ImageView
        android:layout_width="match_parent"
        android:layout_height="match_parent"
        android:scaleType="centerCrop"
        android:src="@drawable/sandy_beach"/>

    <LinearLayout
        android:layout_width="match_parent"
        android:layout_height="match_parent"
        android:gravity="center"
        android:orientation="vertical">

        <fragment
            android:id="@+id/fragment_game"
            class="org.example.tictactoe.GameFragment"
            android:layout_width="wrap_content"
            android:layout_height="wrap_content"
            tools:layout="@layout/fragment_game"/>
        <!-- Control fragment goes here... -->
    </LinearLayout>

</FrameLayout>
```

That's it, except for the Java code that references these layouts.

Starting a Game

Switch over to MainFragment.java for a moment. In the previous chapter we wired up the About button to bring up a dialog. Here, we need to set up the code to start a GameActivity class when the user presses the New or Continue button. Adding the following code to the onCreateView() method in MainFragment.java before the return statement will do the trick:

```
ticTacToev2/src/main/java/org/example/tictactoe/MainFragment.java
View newButton = rootView.findViewById(R.id.new_button);
View continueButton = rootView.findViewById(R.id.continue_button);
newButton.setOnClickListener(new View.OnClickListener() {
  @Override
  public void onClick(View view) {
    Intent intent = new Intent(getActivity(), GameActivity.class);
    getActivity().startActivity(intent);
  }
});
continueButton.setOnClickListener(new View.OnClickListener() {
  @Override
  public void onClick(View view) {
    Intent intent = new Intent(getActivity(), GameActivity.class);
    intent.putExtra(GameActivity.KEY_RESTORE, true);
    getActivity().startActivity(intent);
  }
});
```

This works by first finding the New and Continue buttons in the view hierarchy. Then, we set click listeners on them that will be executed when the user selects the button. The code inside the listener for each button creates a new intent and then starts it. Note that we pass the name of the activity we want to start (GameActivity) since we know it and don't need to search for it.

An intent contains all the parameters needed for an activity when it starts up. In the case of a new game, no parameters are needed. But when continuing a game, we need to pass a flag to indicate the game should continue. To do that, we use the putExtra() method on the intent to set the value of the KEY_RESTORE variable. This will be read when the GameActivity starts up.

Using Alt+Enter

Note that the Intent class is red because we haven't imported it. Click on the word Intent, and press the Alt+Enter keyboard shortcut. The following import will be added automatically near the top of the file and the error will go away:

```
ticTacToev2/src/main/java/org/example/tictactoe/MainFragment.java
import android.content.Intent;
```

You can use the Alt+Enter command to automatically generate missing classes and methods, and to fix many types of errors.

Coding the GameActivity

Here's the outline of the GameActivity class:

ticTacToev2/src/main/java/org/example/tictactoe/GameActivity.java

```java
package org.example.tictactoe;

import android.app.Activity;
import android.app.AlertDialog;
import android.app.Dialog;
import android.content.DialogInterface;
import android.os.Bundle;
import android.util.Log;

public class GameActivity extends Activity {
    @Override
    protected void onCreate(Bundle savedInstanceState) {
        super.onCreate(savedInstanceState);
        setContentView(R.layout.activity_game);
        // Restore game here...
    }
}
```

The onCreate() method is called when the activity starts. It causes its view to be created from the layout/activity_game.xml XML definition we built earlier.

Speaking of XML, every time you add a new activity to an Android program you have to update AndroidManifest.xml to reference it. Simply add these lines before the end of the application block:

ticTacToev2/src/main/AndroidManifest.xml

```xml
<activity
    android:name="org.example.tictactoe.GameActivity">
</activity>
```

The value of the android:name attribute must match the package and class name of the activity in the Java code. If the package name is the same as the package specified in the manifest, you can leave out the package name. But don't remove the dot (".") before the class name.

Continuing a Game

We need a way to continue a game that was already in progress. To do that, we need to add a few lines to the onCreate() method. We also need to declare some new members to GameActivity. Here's the expanded definition:

ticTacToev2/src/main/java/org/example/tictactoe/GameActivity.java

```java
public static final String KEY_RESTORE = "key_restore";
public static final String PREF_RESTORE = "pref_restore";
private GameFragment mGameFragment;

@Override
protected void onCreate(Bundle savedInstanceState) {
    super.onCreate(savedInstanceState);
```

```
    setContentView(R.layout.activity_game);
    // Restore game here...
    mGameFragment = (GameFragment) getFragmentManager()
            .findFragmentById(R.id.fragment_game);
    boolean restore = getIntent().getBooleanExtra(KEY_RESTORE, false);
    if (restore) {
        String gameData = getPreferences(MODE_PRIVATE)
                .getString(PREF_RESTORE, null);
        if (gameData != null) {
            mGameFragment.putState(gameData);
        }
    }
    Log.d("UT3", "restore = " + restore);
}
```

KEY_RESTORE is the name of the flag passed in to the new activity in order to cause the board to be restored from its frozen state. We call the getBooleanExtra() method on the Intent instance that started us to get the value of the flag.

If it's true, then we use the getPreferences() method to get a handle to the Android preferences manager for this activity, and then call getString() to get the value of the PREF_RESTORE item. Preferences are a great way to store small amounts of data persistently. For larger amounts of data, you should use the SQLite database (see Chapter 13, *Putting SQL to Work*, on page 183).

To talk to the game fragment inside the activity, we call getFragmentManager() to get a handle to the object that keeps track of all the fragments, and then call the findFragmentById() method to get a reference to the game fragment. This isn't the only way to do it, or even necessarily the best way, but it's practical and it works. If we were able to get the game state from the preferences, then we could call the fragment's putState() method to change the game state.

When the GameActivity started, it read the state of the game from the preferences. Now let's look at how that was set.

Saving the Game

The behavior we want is this: no matter how the game was stopped, whether it was because we exited to the home screen, started another app, or just pressed the Back button, we want to be able to continue from that point. To do that, we need to save the game every time the activity goes out of the running state (see the lifecycle diagram on page 23).

In that diagram, you will see that the onPause() method is a good place to do the saving. So let's create an onPause() method inside the GameActivity class to add that now (don't forget the Ctrl+Alt+L shortcut to reformat the code to make it more readable):

ticTacToev2/src/main/java/org/example/tictactoe/GameActivity.java

```java
@Override
protected void onPause() {
    super.onPause();
    String gameData = mGameFragment.getState();
    getPreferences(MODE_PRIVATE).edit()
            .putString(PREF_RESTORE, gameData)
            .commit();
    Log.d("UT3", "state = " + gameData);
}
```

First, we call the onPause() method in the superclass, which is Activity.onPause(). You should always call the super's method in any method that overrides a method in the superclass. For all the onXX functions that have something to do with initialization, in general you should call the super's method at the very beginning of the method, but for the ones that are called at termination time, you should call it at the end. If you're not sure, just call it at the beginning.

After that, we call the fragment's getState() method to get the game data. Then we get a handle to the preferences store (getPreferences), create an editor for preferences (edit), save a string under the key PREF_RESTORE (putString), and finally save the changes back to the preferences store (commit). The Log.d() call writes a debugging message to the log.

Restarting the Game

Sometimes we may want to just wipe the slate clean and start over. That's the purpose of the restartGame() method:

ticTacToev2/src/main/java/org/example/tictactoe/GameActivity.java

```java
public void restartGame() {
    mGameFragment.restartGame();
}
```

It simply calls a method of the same name in the fragment class. We'll look at that class in a moment.

Declaring a Winner

Once the winner has been decided we'll need some way to announce that fact. The reportWinner() method takes care of that:

ticTacToev2/src/main/java/org/example/tictactoe/GameActivity.java

```java
public void reportWinner(final Tile.Owner winner) {
    AlertDialog.Builder builder = new AlertDialog.Builder(this);
    builder.setMessage(getString(R.string.declare_winner, winner));
    builder.setCancelable(false);
    builder.setPositiveButton(R.string.ok_label,
```

```
        new DialogInterface.OnClickListener() {
          @Override
          public void onClick(DialogInterface dialogInterface, int i) {
            finish();
          }
        });
    final Dialog dialog = builder.create();
    dialog.show();

    // Reset the board to the initial position
    mGameFragment.initGame();
}
```

This code uses the AlertDialog.Builder class to create a message box containing a single line of text and an OK button. When the user presses OK, the activity will finish—that is, the game screen will close and the user will be returned to the main menu.

Coding the Game Fragment

The GameFragment class is the most complicated class so far because it has to do a lot. First let's define the class outline, including all the imports we need:

```
package org.example.tictactoe;

import android.app.Fragment;
import android.os.Bundle;
import android.util.Log;
import android.view.LayoutInflater;
import android.view.View;
import android.view.ViewGroup;
import android.widget.ImageButton;

import java.util.HashSet;
import java.util.Set;

public class GameFragment extends Fragment {
    // Data structures go here...
    @Override
    public void onCreate(Bundle savedInstanceState) {
        super.onCreate(savedInstanceState);
        // Retain this fragment across configuration changes.
        setRetainInstance(true);
        initGame();
    }
```

```java
    @Override
    public View onCreateView(LayoutInflater inflater, ViewGroup container,
                             Bundle savedInstanceState) {
        View rootView =
            inflater.inflate(R.layout.large_board, container, false);
        initViews(rootView);
        updateAllTiles();
        return rootView;
    }
}
```

There are two important methods. The onCreate() method is called when the fragment is created. We call the setRetainInstance(true) method so that Android won't destroy this fragment when the parent activity is destroyed on a configuration change (such as rotating the device). Then we call a method we'll write called initGame() to set up all our data structures. More on that in a moment.

Although the fragment will live longer than the activity that contained it, the views inside the fragment won't. The purpose of the onCreateView() method is to create (or re-create) those views. First it reads the XML for the large board and turns that into views by calling the LayoutInflater.inflate() method. Then it initializes the views and updates the tiles using two methods that will be defined shortly. See the life-cycle diagram on page 25 for more information on the order in which Android calls fragments methods such as onCreate() and onCreateView().

Data Structures

Before we continue, let's define some data structures in the GameFragment class that we'll need in the other methods. They go inside the class definition at the top:

ticTacToev2/src/main/java/org/example/tictactoe/GameFragment.java
```java
// Data structures go here...
static private int mLargeIds[] = {R.id.large1, R.id.large2, R.id.large3,
    R.id.large4, R.id.large5, R.id.large6, R.id.large7, R.id.large8,
    R.id.large9,};
static private int mSmallIds[] = {R.id.small1, R.id.small2, R.id.small3,
    R.id.small4, R.id.small5, R.id.small6, R.id.small7, R.id.small8,
    R.id.small9,};

private Tile mEntireBoard = new Tile(this);
private Tile mLargeTiles[] = new Tile[9];
private Tile mSmallTiles[][] = new Tile[9][9];
private Tile.Owner mPlayer = Tile.Owner.X;
private Set<Tile> mAvailable = new HashSet<Tile>();
private int mLastLarge;
private int mLastSmall;
```

mLargeIds and mSmallIds are constant arrays that map a number into the resource ids of the large and small tiles, respectively. Remember that large_board.xml and small_board.xml each defined nine subviews in a 3×3 grid. Inside the program we number them 0 through 8. The top row is 0–2, the middle row 3–5, and the bottom 5–8.

mEntireBoard, mLargeTiles, and mSmallTiles represent the game tiles at every level. At the top level there is one tile for the whole game, whereas at the bottom level there are eighty-one tiles where the Xs and Os are placed. The Tile class represents a square on the board at any of the three levels. It will be defined later.

mPlayer holds the id of the player playing right now. X always goes first.

mAvailable is a list of all tiles where it's possible to make a move at any given time. The list will be calculated based on past moves and the game rules.

mLastLarge and mLastSmall are the indexes of the last move. For example, if they are both 4, then the last move was smack-dab in the middle of the board.

Initializing the Game

The initGame() method is called from onCreate() when the fragment is first created. It initializes all the data structures to their starting state.

```
ticTacToev2/src/main/java/org/example/tictactoe/GameFragment.java
public void initGame() {
    Log.d("UT3", "init game");
    mEntireBoard = new Tile(this);
    // Create all the tiles
    for (int large = 0; large < 9; large++) {
        mLargeTiles[large] = new Tile(this);
        for (int small = 0; small < 9; small++) {
            mSmallTiles[large][small] = new Tile(this);
        }
        mLargeTiles[large].setSubTiles(mSmallTiles[large]);
    }
    mEntireBoard.setSubTiles(mLargeTiles);

    // If the player moves first, set which spots are available
    mLastSmall = -1;
    mLastLarge = -1;
    setAvailableFromLastMove(mLastSmall);
}
```

The method creates one tile for the entire board, nine for the large boards, and eighty-one for the small boards. Then it sets up a fake last move and evaluates which moves are available (it should be all of them).

Initializing the Views

Here's how the views are initialized:

ticTacToev2/src/main/java/org/example/tictactoe/GameFragment.java

```java
private void initViews(View rootView) {
  mEntireBoard.setView(rootView);
  for (int large = 0; large < 9; large++) {
    View outer = rootView.findViewById(mLargeIds[large]);
    mLargeTiles[large].setView(outer);

    for (int small = 0; small < 9; small++) {
      ImageButton inner = (ImageButton) outer.findViewById
          (mSmallIds[small]);
      final int fLarge = large;
      final int fSmall = small;
      final Tile smallTile = mSmallTiles[large][small];
      smallTile.setView(inner);
      inner.setOnClickListener(new View.OnClickListener() {
        @Override
        public void onClick(View view) {
          if (isAvailable(smallTile)) {
            makeMove(fLarge, fSmall);
            switchTurns();
          }
        }
      });
    }
  }
}
```

We start with the large (outer) boards, then work our way to the small (inner) boards. After setting the view for each board, we set the click handler that will be called when the user touches the tile. If the tile is a valid move, we make that the move and then switch sides to give the other player a turn.

Making a Move

To make a move, we call the makeMove() method, passing it the index of the large and small tile to which we're moving:

ticTacToev2/src/main/java/org/example/tictactoe/GameFragment.java

```java
private void makeMove(int large, int small) {
  mLastLarge = large;
  mLastSmall = small;
  Tile smallTile = mSmallTiles[large][small];
  Tile largeTile = mLargeTiles[large];
  smallTile.setOwner(mPlayer);
  setAvailableFromLastMove(small);
  Tile.Owner oldWinner = largeTile.getOwner();
  Tile.Owner winner = largeTile.findWinner();
```

```
    if (winner != oldWinner) {
        largeTile.setOwner(winner);
    }
    winner = mEntireBoard.findWinner();
    mEntireBoard.setOwner(winner);
    updateAllTiles();
    if (winner != Tile.Owner.NEITHER) {
        ((GameActivity)getActivity()).reportWinner(winner);
    }
}
```

The main thing to do is set the owner of the small tile to the current player. After that, we need to figure out if anyone has won the board containing the small tile. If so, we set its owner. Finally, we look at the entire board to see if that has an owner now. That would mean someone has won the game, so when that happens we call a method to report the winner to the user.

Switching Turns

Switching turns is as easy as toggling the value of the mPlayer variable.

ticTacToev2/src/main/java/org/example/tictactoe/GameFragment.java
```
private void switchTurns() {
    mPlayer = mPlayer == Tile.Owner.X ? Tile.Owner.O : Tile
            .Owner.X;
}
```

If the player is currently X, we set it to O; otherwise we set it to X.

Restarting the Game

When the user selects the restart button, the listener calls the restartGame() method in GameActivity, which in turn calls restartGame() in the game fragment.

ticTacToev2/src/main/java/org/example/tictactoe/GameFragment.java
```
public void restartGame() {
    initGame();
    initViews(getView());
    updateAllTiles();
}
```

First, it initializes the game state as if we were first starting up. Then it initializes the views again and updates all the tiles so they'll be drawn correctly.

Handling Available Moves

According to the rules of Ultimate Tic-Tac-Toe, when a player makes a move, it forces the opponent to move in the large board that has the same coordinate as the small board picked by the player. For example, if Player 1 marks the top-left tile of any small board, then Player 2's move has to be somewhere in the top-left large board. If there are no moves available (that is, the small board is full), then the second player can move anywhere.

Several methods are used to keep track of which moves are valid or available at any given time, based on the previous move.

```
ticTacToev2/src/main/java/org/example/tictactoe/GameFragment.java
private void clearAvailable() {
    mAvailable.clear();
}

private void addAvailable(Tile tile) {
    mAvailable.add(tile);
}

public boolean isAvailable(Tile tile) {
    return mAvailable.contains(tile);
}

private void setAvailableFromLastMove(int small) {
    clearAvailable();
    // Make all the tiles at the destination available
    if (small != -1) {
        for (int dest = 0; dest < 9; dest++) {
            Tile tile = mSmallTiles[small][dest];
            if (tile.getOwner() == Tile.Owner.NEITHER)
                addAvailable(tile);
        }
    }
    // If there were none available, make all squares available
    if (mAvailable.isEmpty()) {
        setAllAvailable();
    }
}

private void setAllAvailable() {
    for (int large = 0; large < 9; large++) {
        for (int small = 0; small < 9; small++) {
            Tile tile = mSmallTiles[large][small];
            if (tile.getOwner() == Tile.Owner.NEITHER)
                addAvailable(tile);
        }
    }
}
```

clearAvailable() clears the available list so more can be added, addAvailable() adds one tile to the list of available tiles, and isAvailable() checks to see if the specified tile is available for a move. setAvailableFromLastMove() clears the available list and then marks unoccupied tiles at the available large board as available. Finally, setAllAvailable() is called if there are no possible moves in the destination board. It marks all unoccupied tiles in all boards as available.

Handling State

In order to save the game and continue it later, we need a way to get the current state of the game into a serialized form (a string) so we can save it in the preferences. Here's the code to create the string:

ticTacToev2/src/main/java/org/example/tictactoe/GameFragment.java

```java
/** Create a string containing the state of the game. */
public String getState() {
   StringBuilder builder = new StringBuilder();
   builder.append(mLastLarge);
   builder.append(',');
   builder.append(mLastSmall);
   builder.append(',');
   for (int large = 0; large < 9; large++) {
      for (int small = 0; small < 9; small++) {
         builder.append(mSmallTiles[large][small].getOwner().name());
         builder.append(',');
      }
   }
   return builder.toString();
}
```

The most important thing is the owner of each small tile, but we also have to keep track of the last move. That's because the available moves on the next turn are determined by the move on the last turn.

Once we have the string and save it in preferences, we can extract it and "deserialize" it into a new game state. That's done with the putState() method:

ticTacToev2/src/main/java/org/example/tictactoe/GameFragment.java

```java
/** Restore the state of the game from the given string. */
public void putState(String gameData) {
   String[] fields = gameData.split(",");
   int index = 0;
   mLastLarge = Integer.parseInt(fields[index++]);
   mLastSmall = Integer.parseInt(fields[index++]);
   for (int large = 0; large < 9; large++) {
      for (int small = 0; small < 9; small++) {
         Tile.Owner owner = Tile.Owner.valueOf(fields[index++]);
         mSmallTiles[large][small].setOwner(owner);
      }
   }
   setAvailableFromLastMove(mLastSmall);
   updateAllTiles();
}
```

Basically it's the opposite of getState(). We get the last move and the owner of each tile, and store them in member variables. At the end, we recalculate the list of available moves and update the drawable state of all tiles.

Something is missing from the serialized game state. For extra credit, can you figure out what it is?

Here's the code to update the drawable states:

ticTacToev2/src/main/java/org/example/tictactoe/GameFragment.java
```java
private void updateAllTiles() {
   mEntireBoard.updateDrawableState();
   for (int large = 0; large < 9; large++) {
      mLargeTiles[large].updateDrawableState();
      for (int small = 0; small < 9; small++) {
         mSmallTiles[large][small].updateDrawableState();
      }
   }
}
```

The code updates the state of the tile representing the overall board, then each of the large tiles for the nine first-level boards, and finally each of the small tiles that contain the individual Xs and Os.

Defining the Tile Class

The Tile class represents one tile at any level of the game. It could be the lowest level where you place the Xs and Os, or it could be the small board containing nine other tiles, or it could be the large board containing nine small boards.

Here's the outline of the Tile class:

ticTacToev2/src/main/java/org/example/tictactoe/Tile.java
```java
package org.example.tictactoe;

import android.graphics.drawable.Drawable;
import android.view.View;
import android.widget.ImageButton;

public class Tile {

   public enum Owner {
      X, O /* letter O */, NEITHER, BOTH
   }

   // These levels are defined in the drawable definitions
   private static final int LEVEL_X = 0;
   private static final int LEVEL_O = 1; // letter O
   private static final int LEVEL_BLANK = 2;
   private static final int LEVEL_AVAILABLE = 3;
```

```
    private static final int LEVEL_TIE = 3;

    private final GameFragment mGame;
    private Owner mOwner = Owner.NEITHER;
    private View mView;
    private Tile mSubTiles[];

    public Tile(GameFragment game) {
        this.mGame = game;
    }

    public View getView() {
        return mView;
    }

    public void setView(View view) {
        this.mView = view;
    }

    public Owner getOwner() {
        return mOwner;
    }

    public void setOwner(Owner owner) {
        this.mOwner = owner;
    }

    public Tile[] getSubTiles() {
        return mSubTiles;
    }

    public void setSubTiles(Tile[] subTiles) {
        this.mSubTiles = subTiles;
    }
}
```

A tile has an owner, a view (its graphical representation), and possibly a set of sub-tiles. The class has a Tile constructor, plus getters and setters for the owner, view, and sub-tiles. In addition, it contains code to manage the drawable state and code to decide who the winner is after a move was made. Let's look at the drawable code next. This should be placed inside the Tile class before the closing curly brace:

ticTacToev2/src/main/java/org/example/tictactoe/Tile.java
```
public void updateDrawableState() {
    if (mView == null) return;
    int level = getLevel();
    if (mView.getBackground() != null) {
        mView.getBackground().setLevel(level);
    }
```

```java
    if (mView instanceof ImageButton) {
        Drawable drawable = ((ImageButton) mView).getDrawable();
        drawable.setLevel(level);
    }
}

private int getLevel() {
    int level = LEVEL_BLANK;
    switch (mOwner) {
        case X:
            level = LEVEL_X;
            break;
        case O: // letter O
            level = LEVEL_O;
            break;
        case BOTH:
            level = LEVEL_TIE;
            break;
        case NEITHER:
            level = mGame.isAvailable(this) ? LEVEL_AVAILABLE : LEVEL_BLANK;
            break;
    }
    return level;
}
```

Remember from *Starting Small*, on page 53 that a small tile has four levels depending on the owner: X, O, both, and neither. The updateDrawableState() method calls getLevel() to figure that out. Then it calls the setLevel() method on either the view background or drawable depending on the type of view.

Next we need some code to find the winner of a tile:

ticTacToev2/src/main/java/org/example/tictactoe/Tile.java
```java
public Owner findWinner() {
    // If owner already calculated, return it
    if (getOwner() != Owner.NEITHER)
        return getOwner();

    int totalX[] = new int[4];
    int totalO[] = new int[4];
    countCaptures(totalX, totalO);
    if (totalX[3] > 0) return Owner.X;
    if (totalO[3] > 0) return Owner.O;

    // Check for a draw
    int total = 0;
    for (int row = 0; row < 3; row++) {
        for (int col = 0; col < 3; col++) {
            Owner owner = mSubTiles[3 * row + col].getOwner();
            if (owner != Owner.NEITHER) total++;
```

```
        }
        if (total == 9) return Owner.BOTH;
    }

    // Neither player has won this tile
    return Owner.NEITHER;
}
```

If the tile already has an owner, then we've already determined the winner so we return that. Otherwise we count the number of tiles captured by both players. If one of them has captured three in a row, then that's the winner. Otherwise we check to see if all the tiles in the sub-board have been captured. If they have, then we have a tie and return BOTH. Otherwise neither player has won the tile, so we return NEITHER.

Here's the definition of the countCaptures() method:

ticTacToev2/src/main/java/org/example/tictactoe/Tile.java
```
private void countCaptures(int totalX[], int totalO[]) {
    int capturedX, capturedO;
    // Check the horizontal
    for (int row = 0; row < 3; row++) {
        capturedX = capturedO = 0;
        for (int col = 0; col < 3; col++) {
            Owner owner = mSubTiles[3 * row + col].getOwner();
            if (owner == Owner.X || owner == Owner.BOTH) capturedX++;
            if (owner == Owner.O || owner == Owner.BOTH) capturedO++;
        }
        totalX[capturedX]++;
        totalO[capturedO]++;
    }

    // Check the vertical
    for (int col = 0; col < 3; col++) {
        capturedX = capturedO = 0;
        for (int row = 0; row < 3; row++) {
            Owner owner = mSubTiles[3 * row + col].getOwner();
            if (owner == Owner.X || owner == Owner.BOTH) capturedX++;
            if (owner == Owner.O || owner == Owner.BOTH) capturedO++;
        }
        totalX[capturedX]++;
        totalO[capturedO]++;
    }

    // Check the diagonals
    capturedX = capturedO = 0;
    for (int diag = 0; diag < 3; diag++) {
        Owner owner = mSubTiles[3 * diag + diag].getOwner();
        if (owner == Owner.X || owner == Owner.BOTH) capturedX++;
        if (owner == Owner.O || owner == Owner.BOTH) capturedO++;
```

```
    }
    totalX[capturedX]++;
    totalO[capturedO]++;
    capturedX = capturedO = 0;
    for (int diag = 0; diag < 3; diag++) {
        Owner owner = mSubTiles[3 * diag + (2 - diag)].getOwner();
        if (owner == Owner.X || owner == Owner.BOTH) capturedX++;
        if (owner == Owner.O || owner == Owner.BOTH) capturedO++;
    }
    totalX[capturedX]++;
    totalO[capturedO]++;
}
```

It looks like a lot of code but it's very simple. First we count the Xs and Os on all the horizontal rows; then we count them on the vertical columns, and finally on the two diagonals. The results are returned in two arrays: totalX for player X and totalO for player O.

Controlling the Game

While playing the game, the user might want to start over or go back to the main menu. Of course, users can press the Back button to go back, but since some people have trouble finding the Back button we'll provide a way to return on screen.

Let's start with a fragment containing a button for "Restart" and one for "Main Menu":

ticTacToev2/src/main/res/layout/fragment_control.xml
```xml
<LinearLayout
    xmlns:android="http://schemas.android.com/apk/res/android"
    xmlns:tools="http://schemas.android.com/tools"
    android:layout_width="wrap_content"
    android:layout_height="wrap_content"
    android:orientation="horizontal"
    android:padding="@dimen/control_padding"
    tools:context=".GameActivity">

    <Button
        android:id="@+id/button_restart"
        android:layout_width="match_parent"
        android:layout_height="wrap_content"
        android:elevation="@dimen/elevation_low"
        android:drawableTop="@drawable/restart"
        android:text="@string/restart_label"/>

    <Button
        android:id="@+id/button_main"
        android:layout_width="match_parent"
```

```
   android:layout_height="wrap_content"
   android:elevation="@dimen/elevation_low"
   android:drawableTop="@drawable/home"
   android:text="@string/main_menu_label"/>
```

```
</LinearLayout>
```

The two images can be placed in any of the drawable directories. I drew them with a paint program and put them in res/drawable-xxhdpi/home.png and res/drawable-xxhdpi/restart.png along with a pretty background image for the GameActivity in res/drawable-xxhdpi/sandy_beach.jpg. You can find all these images in the code examples zip file on the book's website.

Next we need to include the new fragment in our GameActivity:

ticTacToev2/src/main/res/layout/activity_game.xml
```xml
<!-- Control fragment goes here... -->
<fragment
   android:id="@+id/fragment_game_controls"
   class="org.example.tictactoe.ControlFragment"
   android:layout_width="wrap_content"
   android:layout_height="wrap_content"
   tools:layout="@layout/fragment_control"/>
```

Finally, we need a bit of Java code to go with the layout:

ticTacToev2/src/main/java/org/example/tictactoe/ControlFragment.java
```java
package org.example.tictactoe;

import android.app.Fragment;
import android.os.Bundle;
import android.view.LayoutInflater;
import android.view.View;
import android.view.ViewGroup;

public class ControlFragment extends Fragment {

   @Override
   public View onCreateView(LayoutInflater inflater, ViewGroup container,
                            Bundle savedInstanceState) {
      View rootView =
           inflater.inflate(R.layout.fragment_control, container, false);
      View main = rootView.findViewById(R.id.button_main);
      View restart = rootView.findViewById(R.id.button_restart);

      main.setOnClickListener(new View.OnClickListener() {
        @Override
        public void onClick(View view) {
           getActivity().finish();
        }
      });
```

```
        restart.setOnClickListener(new View.OnClickListener() {
            @Override
            public void onClick(View view) {
                ((GameActivity) getActivity()).restartGame();
            }
        });
        return rootView;
    }
}
```

The main menu button finishes the current activity. This is the same as pressing Back.

The restart button makes the assumption that the control fragment is embedded in the GameActivity, casts the current activity to GameActivity, and calls the method to restart the game that we defined earlier.

Super-Size Me

In this chapter, we've added a few more dimensions and colors. Let's define them now so we can get rid of all those errors. First, the dimensions:

ticTacToev2/src/main/res/values/dimens.xml
```
<dimen name="activity_horizontal_margin">8dp</dimen>
<dimen name="activity_vertical_margin">8dp</dimen>
<dimen name="tile_size">30dp</dimen>
<dimen name="tile_margin">0dp</dimen>
<dimen name="tile_padding">3dp</dimen>
<dimen name="control_padding">20dp</dimen>
<dimen name="small_board_padding">2dp</dimen>
<dimen name="small_board_margin">2dp</dimen>
<dimen name="elevation_low">4dp</dimen>
```

You may be wondering how I came up all the values for margins, tile sizes, and other dimensions. I could've gotten out the graph paper and planned it all out, but the truth is I just tweaked and refined it until it looked good. Not everything is rocket science.

Next comes the colors:

ticTacToev2/src/main/res/values/colors.xml
```
<color name="dark_border_color">#4f4f4f</color>
<color name="available_color">#7fbf7f</color>
<color name="blue_color">#7f7fff</color>
<color name="gray_color">#bfbfbf</color>
<color name="purple_color">#7f007f</color>
<color name="red_color">#ff7f7f</color>
```

I chose the values for all these colors to look nice with the background image and with the X and O colors.

And don't forget the strings:

ticTacToev2/src/main/res/values/strings.xml

```xml
<string name="restart_label">Restart</string>
<string name="main_menu_label">Main Menu</string>
<string name="declare_winner">%1$s is the winner</string>
```

While we're at it, let's define a landscape version of the GameActivity and control fragment. These will be used when the display is turned on its side. They're identical to the portrait versions but rearranged so they appear better on a wide screen.

ticTacToev2/src/main/res/layout-land/activity_game.xml

```xml
<FrameLayout
    xmlns:android="http://schemas.android.com/apk/res/android"
    xmlns:tools="http://schemas.android.com/tools"
    android:layout_width="match_parent"
    android:layout_height="match_parent"
    tools:context=".TicTacToeActivity">

    <ImageView
        android:layout_width="match_parent"
        android:layout_height="match_parent"
        android:scaleType="centerCrop"
        android:src="@drawable/sandy_beach"/>

    <LinearLayout
        android:layout_width="match_parent"
        android:layout_height="match_parent"
        android:gravity="center"
        android:baselineAligned="false"
        android:orientation="horizontal">

        <fragment
            android:id="@+id/fragment_game"
            class="org.example.tictactoe.GameFragment"
            android:layout_width="wrap_content"
            android:layout_height="wrap_content"
            tools:layout="@layout/fragment_game"/>

        <fragment
            android:id="@+id/fragment_game_controls"
            class="org.example.tictactoe.ControlFragment"
            android:layout_width="wrap_content"
            android:layout_height="wrap_content"
            tools:layout="@layout/fragment_control"/>
    </LinearLayout>

</FrameLayout>
```

ticTacToev2/src/main/res/layout-land/fragment_control.xml

```
<LinearLayout
    xmlns:android="http://schemas.android.com/apk/res/android"
    xmlns:tools="http://schemas.android.com/tools"
    android:layout_width="wrap_content"
    android:layout_height="wrap_content"
    android:orientation="vertical"
    android:padding="@dimen/control_padding"
    tools:context=".GameActivity">

    <Button
        android:id="@+id/button_restart"
        android:layout_width="match_parent"
        android:layout_height="wrap_content"
        android:drawableTop="@drawable/restart"
        android:elevation="@dimen/elevation_low"
        android:text="@string/restart_label"/>

    <Button
        android:id="@+id/button_main"
        android:layout_width="match_parent"
        android:layout_height="wrap_content"
        android:drawableTop="@drawable/home"
        android:elevation="@dimen/elevation_low"
        android:text="@string/main_menu_label"/>

</LinearLayout>
```

Note they go in the res/layout-land directory. The -land suffix indicates landscape mode.

At this point you should be able to run the game and play it by taking turns until one player wins. Find a friend and try it out. I think you'll find that it's not as easy to win as you might think.

If you run into trouble, think of it as a learning experience. Get any compiler errors out first, and then refer to *Debugging*, on page 48 for help with runtime errors such as exceptions and blank screens.

As a last resort, you can download the code from the book's website and compare it to what you have. After downloading and extracting the zip file, right-click on the app folder in the Project window and select "Compare Directory with..."; then browse to the src directory inside the ticTacToev2 example and click OK.

Fast-Forward >>

In this chapter you learned how to build a user interface from the ground up, starting with the smallest unit (a tile) and building your way up to a small and large board. You included layouts from within other layouts, and defined styles to keep from repeating yourself. And you saw one way of communicating between fragments and activities.

The next chapter will add an AI to the game so it can play you (badly). If you want to skip that part, just copy the code from the website and move on to the chapters on animation (Chapter 7, *Adding Animation*, on page 101) and multimedia (Chapter 6, *Adding Sounds*, on page 93).

CHAPTER 5

Ghost in the Machine

So far we've created a game that lets the user make moves by touching the screen and alternating between the X and O players. In this chapter we're going to turn Tic-Tac-Toe into a single-player game, where the human makes a move and the computer responds.

To do this, we need to teach the app how to evaluate positions on the game board and choose the best move from all the ones available. This will require that we take a quick detour into the world of AI (artificial intelligence).

Introduction to AI

AI plays a role in almost any kind of game you might want to write, and some non-game programs as well. For example, AI techniques are used to build smart apps that anticipate the user's actions and learn based on heuristics and past behavior. Because users tend to project their own abilities into that of the program, it doesn't take much to achieve the appearance of intelligence.

How AIs Work

Over the years, computer scientists have developed a number of ways to teach computers how to play games. One of the simplest is the *minimax* algorithm, named because it alternately tries to minimize or maximize the score depending on whose turn it is.

Gameplay is broken down into a sequence of *plys*, or half-turns. When the human moves, that's one ply; when the computer moves, that's another.

The minimax algorithm is called during the computer's turn. It evaluates each possible move by assigning a number to the resulting position. This is the first ply. We'll arbitrarily use positive numbers for positions favorable to the human and negative numbers for positions favorable to the computer. So at this point, the best move is the one with the lowest number.

Next, for all those moves, the computer looks at the possible moves by the human and evaluates all those positions. This is the second ply. Naturally the human will want to pick the best position for them, so the most likely move at the second stage is the one that has the highest number.

The algorithm continues for as long as possible. As you can imagine, it won't be able to look ahead very many moves because each ply multiplies the number of combinations by the number of available moves on that ply. So, for example, if there are five moves on the first ply, and after each of those there are five moves, and five possible moves after that, we're already up to $5 \times 5 \times 5 = 125$ possible positions that have to be evaluated. Trying to evaluate only fourteen plies (seven turns) ahead would mean billions of positions. Usually there's a limit on the amount of time that the computer is allowed to think, so at some point it has to cut off and take the best result.

Techniques such as alpha-beta pruning[1] and Negamax[2] are available to limit the amount of work, but they're beyond the scope of this book. In fact, for this example we're going to evaluate only one ply.

Evaluating the Board

Humans can look at the board and get a feel for how good or bad it is, but computers don't deal in feelings; they only understand numbers. How do you turn a board position into a number? That's the job of an evaluation function. Creating a good evaluation function is key to game AI. Take a look at this one:

ticTacToev3/src/main/java/org/example/tictactoe/Tile.java
```java
public int evaluate() {
    switch (getOwner()) {
        case X:
            return 100;
        case O:
            return -100;
        case NEITHER:
            int total = 0;
            if (getSubTiles() != null) {
                for (int tile = 0; tile < 9; tile++) {
                    total += getSubTiles()[tile].evaluate();
                }
```

---

1. http://en.wikipedia.org/wiki/Alpha-beta_pruning
2. http://en.wikipedia.org/wiki/Negamax

```
        int totalX[] = new int[4];
        int totalO[] = new int[4];
        countCaptures(totalX, totalO);
        total = total * 100 + totalX[1] + 2 * totalX[2] + 8 *
                totalX[3] - totalO[1] - 2 * totalO[2] - 8 * totalO[3];
    }
    return total;
    }
    return 0;
}
```

Tiles are arranged hierarchically. Starting from the top, there's one tile that represents the entire board. That tile has nine children, representing the nine large boards of the game. Each of those tiles has nine children, one for each of the small tiles. The final level of tiles doesn't have any children because it contains either an X or an O.

If X or O already owns the tile, the evaluation function just returns a large number. The interesting case is when neither one owns the tile. For that, we have to look down one level.

First we evaluate each sub-tile and total up all the scores. Then we count the number of captures in the sub-tiles and compute a formula based on that. For X, we give each 3-in-a-row 8 points, each 2-in-a-row 2 points, and each singleton 1 point. Then we take away the same amount for captures by O.

The formula and numbers in the evaluation function are completely arbitrary. As an exercise for you, you can try to come up with a better one. It shouldn't be too hard.

Simulating Thought

In a real game we'd look ahead several plys until we either reached the end of the game (a win, loss, or draw) or a timer ran out. For this example, we'll use a timer to simulate one second of think time.

Using a Handler and postDelayed

To start, we need to declare and initialize an Android Handler instance in GameFragment.java:

ticTacToev3/src/main/java/org/example/tictactoe/GameFragment.java
```
import android.os.Handler;
public class GameFragment extends Fragment {
    // Data structures go here...
    private Handler mHandler = new Handler();
    // ...
}
```

A handler is a class that lets us delay doing something until later. We call its postDelayed() method, passing it the code that we want to run when the timer expires, and then the number of milliseconds to wait. Importantly, the code will be run on the main user interface thread, so it can manipulate views on the screen.

To use it, first let's change the click listener to call a new method called think():

ticTacToev3/src/main/java/org/example/tictactoe/GameFragment.java
```
private void initViews(View rootView) {
        // ...
        inner.setOnClickListener(new View.OnClickListener() {
          @Override
          public void onClick(View view) {
            if (isAvailable(smallTile)) {
                makeMove(fLarge, fSmall);
                think();
            }
          }
        });
        // ...
}
```

Here's the definition of the think() method:

ticTacToev3/src/main/java/org/example/tictactoe/GameFragment.java
```
private void think() {
   ((GameActivity)getActivity()).startThinking();
   mHandler.postDelayed(new Runnable() {
     @Override
     public void run() {
        if (getActivity() == null) return;
        if (mEntireBoard.getOwner() == Tile.Owner.NEITHER) {
           int move[] = new int[2];
           pickMove(move);
           if (move[0] != -1 && move[1] != -1) {
              switchTurns();
              makeMove(move[0], move[1]);
              switchTurns();
           }
        }
        ((GameActivity) getActivity()).stopThinking();
     }
   }, 1000);
}
```

When the user taps a tile, we turn on the thinking indicator, make the move requested by the user, and then start the timer. 1000 milliseconds (1 second) later, the run() method will execute.

Assuming the activity wasn't closed while we were waiting and the game didn't end yet, we pick a move and make it. Then we stop the thinking indicator. That's all there is to it! Well, mostly...

Blocking Input while Thinking

The first time I wrote this app, the game worked fine until I started tapping the board a little too fast, which caused the program to crash. The reason was that I was tapping tiles and buttons during the think time, and code was being run out of order. How can we prevent that?

One way is to add checks everywhere that accept input to see if we're currently thinking and disallow or queue up the tap. An easier way is just to block all input. We can do that with a clever use of the thinking indicator. Instead of making a small indicator in the corner, we make a large view that covers the entire screen and intercepts all taps. Then we put the spinning indicator in the corner of that. The rest of the view is transparent. Here's what we want our user to see while the game is deep in thought:

Here's the layout of the thinking view:

ticTacToev3/src/main/res/layout/thinking.xml

```xml
<?xml version="1.0" encoding="utf-8"?>
<FrameLayout
    xmlns:android="http://schemas.android.com/apk/res/android"
    xmlns:tools="http://schemas.android.com/tools"
    android:id="@+id/thinking"
    android:layout_width="match_parent"
    android:layout_height="match_parent"
    android:clickable="true"
    android:visibility="gone"
    tools:showIn="@layout/game_activity">
```

```
<ProgressBar
    android:background="@drawable/thinking_background"
    android:elevation="@dimen/elevation_high"
    android:layout_marginTop="@dimen/activity_vertical_margin"
    android:layout_marginLeft="@dimen/activity_vertical_margin"
    android:layout_width="@dimen/thinking_progress_size"
    android:layout_height="@dimen/thinking_progress_size"
    android:indeterminate="true"/>
</FrameLayout>
```

Add this line to the GameActivity layout, before the ending FrameLayout tag:

ticTacToev3/src/main/res/layout/activity_game.xml
```
<include layout="@layout/thinking"/>
```

The background of the progress bar will be an oval:

ticTacToev3/src/main/res/drawable/thinking_background.xml
```
<?xml version="1.0" encoding="utf-8"?>
<shape
    xmlns:android="http://schemas.android.com/apk/res/android"
    android:shape="oval">

    <solid android:color="@color/thinking_background_color"/>
</shape>
```

Now we can use this in the GameActivity:

ticTacToev3/src/main/java/org/example/tictactoe/GameActivity.java
```
import android.view.View;

public class GameActivity extends Activity {
    // ...
    public void startThinking() {
        View thinkView = findViewById(R.id.thinking);
        thinkView.setVisibility(View.VISIBLE);
    }

    public void stopThinking() {
        View thinkView = findViewById(R.id.thinking);
        thinkView.setVisibility(View.GONE);
    }
}
```

There are two methods: startThinking() and stopThinking(). Both look up the thinking view that we added in activity_game.xml, and then set it to either visible or gone. *Gone* is like invisible except it doesn't get any events or participate in the layout.

Making Your Move

Selecting which move to make next is a matter of looking at all the possible moves and evaluating each position. Then we go with the choice that gives the lowest score. (Remember, low means good for the computer.)

Picking the Right Move

Here's the code to add to GameFragment.java to pick the next move:

```
ticTacToev3/src/main/java/org/example/tictactoe/GameFragment.java
private void pickMove(int move[]) {
    Tile.Owner opponent = mPlayer == Tile.Owner.X ? Tile.Owner.O : Tile
            .Owner.X;
    int bestLarge = -1;
    int bestSmall = -1;
    int bestValue = Integer.MAX_VALUE;
    for (int large = 0; large < 9; large++) {
        for (int small = 0; small < 9; small++) {
            Tile smallTile = mSmallTiles[large][small];
            if (isAvailable(smallTile)) {
                // Try the move and get the score
                Tile newBoard = mEntireBoard.deepCopy();
                newBoard.getSubTiles()[large].getSubTiles()[small]
                        .setOwner(opponent);
                int value = newBoard.evaluate();
                Log.d("UT3",
                        "Moving to " + large + ", " + small + " gives value " +
                                "" + value
                );
                if (value < bestValue) {
                    bestLarge = large;
                    bestSmall = small;
                    bestValue = value;
                }
            }
        }
    }
    move[0] = bestLarge;
    move[1] = bestSmall;
    Log.d("UT3", "Best move is " + bestLarge + ", " + bestSmall);
}
```

We run through every small tile (all eighty-one of them) and use the isAvailable() method to see whether that's a valid move. If it's valid, then we make a copy of the board, make the move in the copy by calling setOwner(), and evaluate. As we go, we keep track of the best value we got from the evaluation function along with the move that produced it. Once we're done with the loop, we return the move in the provided arrays (that's a little Java idiom to return multiple values).

Here's the code to make a copy of the board. It goes in Tile.java:

```
ticTacToev3/src/main/java/org/example/tictactoe/Tile.java
public Tile deepCopy() {
    Tile tile = new Tile(mGame);
    tile.setOwner(getOwner());
    if (getSubTiles() != null) {
        Tile newTiles[] = new Tile[9];
        Tile oldTiles[] = getSubTiles();
        for (int child = 0; child < 9; child++) {
            newTiles[child] = oldTiles[child].deepCopy();
        }
        tile.setSubTiles(newTiles);
    }
    return tile;
}
```

We start by creating a new tile and copying the owner. Then we check to see if there are any sub-tiles. If there are, we create a new array of tile references to hold our copy, then recursively call deepCopy() on each child. Finally, we set the sub-tiles reference to the new array. If the original tile didn't have any sub-tiles (in other words, it was a leaf node that just contained an X or O), then there's nothing else to do.

Colors and Dimensions

If you look back over the example code we've entered so far, you'll see a couple of references to colors and sizes. You can make up whatever values you like that look good, but here are the ones I used.

The background used for the thinking indicator is a light gray:

```
ticTacToev3/src/main/res/values/colors.xml
<color name="thinking_background_color">#cfdfdfdf</color>
```

The size of the indicator is set in res/values/dimens.xml:

```
ticTacToev3/src/main/res/values/dimens.xml
<dimen name="thinking_progress_size">50dp</dimen>
```

The indicator itself is medium-sized, designed not to be too distracting when tucked in the corner of the screen, but big enough to be seen on most devices.

Fast-Forward >>

In this chapter we added the ability for the game to make its own moves. We explored a little game theory, and made a visual indicator when the game was thinking. The next two chapters will wrap up the Tic-Tac-Toe example by adding animation and sounds. If that doesn't interest you, you can skip to Chapter 8, *Write Once, Test Everywhere*, on page 113, where you'll learn how to make your apps run on any kind of device.

CHAPTER 6

Adding Sounds

Remember those Apple television ads with the silhouette people dancing wildly to the beat of their iPods? That's the kind of excitement you want your products to generate. (Of course, normal people older than the age of 18 can't dance like that...except perhaps that time when my kids put a lizard in my...well, I digress.) Music and sound effects can make your programs more immersive and engaging than text and graphics alone.

This chapter will show you how to add multimedia to your Android application. You may not have your users cavorting in the aisles, but if you do it properly, you can at least put smiles on their faces.

The Sound of Music

It was a dark and stormy night.... There goes the starting shot, and they're off.... The crowd goes wild as State sinks a three-pointer with one second remaining....

Audio cues permeate the environment and set the tempo for our emotions. Think of sound as another way to get into your user's head. Just like you use graphics on the display to convey some information to the user, you can use audio to back that up and reinforce it.

Android supports music output through the MediaPlayer class in the android.media package.[1] Let's try it by adding some background music to the opening scene in the Tic-Tac-Toe game.

First we need some music. You can use whatever you like, but a great place to find audio is a site called freesound.org.[2] You can search for specific types

---

1.   http://d.android.com/guide/topics/media
2.   http://www.freesound.org

and genres, play samples, download the ones you like, and use them in your apps. Be sure to follow the copyright licenses for each piece you use if you distribute the app, especially for commercial purposes.

For the opening music, I chose a piece called "epicbuilduploop," created by a user named a_guy_1. The audio was originally in MP3 format. Android can play MP3, but if you're going to do a looping sound (one that repeats over and over) or the clip is very short then I've found that the OGG format works best because the start and stop points are more precise. Therefore I used a program called Audacity[3] to edit and convert all the sounds used in this example. You can find all the converted music and sound effects in the tic-TacToev4 example code on the book's website.[4]

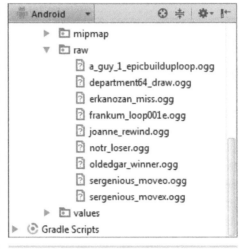

Figure 3—Music and sound effects go in the raw directory.

Once you have your music picked out and converted, put it in the res/raw directory, creating the directory if necessary. For example, I put mine in res/raw/a_guy_1_epicbuilduploop.ogg. The figure shows how it should look in your Android Studio project.

Next, modify the main activity to start and stop the music:

```
ticTacToev4/src/main/java/org/example/tictactoe/MainActivity.java
import android.media.MediaPlayer;

public class MainActivity extends Activity {
    MediaPlayer mMediaPlayer;
    // ...
    @Override
    protected void onResume() {
        super.onResume();
        mMediaPlayer = MediaPlayer.create(this, R.raw.a_guy_1_epicbuilduploop);
        mMediaPlayer.setVolume(0.5f, 0.5f);
        mMediaPlayer.setLooping(true);
        mMediaPlayer.start();
    }
```

---

3. http://audacity.sourceforge.net
4. http://pragprog.com/book/eband4

```
    @Override
    protected void onPause() {
        super.onPause();
        mMediaPlayer.stop();
        mMediaPlayer.reset();
        mMediaPlayer.release();
    }
}
```

The onResume() method is called when the activity becomes visible. We create a media player, passing it the resource id for the file in res/raw; reduce its volume a bit; set it to looping; and start the player.

When the user switches out of the activity, either by going to the next screen, exiting the program, or starting another app, Android calls onPause(), where we stop the music and release any resources the player might have allocated. Failing to do that last step will result in a memory leak and eventually a crash.

Try the game now and you should hear a song playing during the main screen. It gets annoying after a while, so press the Back button or start a new game to make it go away.

Music to Play By

Playing a different song during the game would be a nice change of pace, so let's make a similar change to GameActivity.java. While we're there, we'll add a sound that plays when the game is over. First we need to declare the variable for the media player and a handler we'll need later:

ticTacToev4/src/main/java/org/example/tictactoe/GameActivity.java
```
import android.media.MediaPlayer;
import android.os.Handler;

public class GameActivity extends Activity {
    private MediaPlayer mMediaPlayer;
    private Handler mHandler = new Handler();
    // ...
}
```

Then we start and stop the music in onResume() and onPause() as before:

ticTacToev4/src/main/java/org/example/tictactoe/GameActivity.java
```
@Override
protected void onResume() {
    super.onResume();
    mMediaPlayer = MediaPlayer.create(this, R.raw.frankum_loop001e);
    mMediaPlayer.setLooping(true);
    mMediaPlayer.start();
}
```

```
@Override
protected void onPause() {
    super.onPause();
    mHandler.removeCallbacks(null);
    mMediaPlayer.stop();
    mMediaPlayer.reset();
    mMediaPlayer.release();
    String gameData = mGameFragment.getState();
    getPreferences(MODE_PRIVATE).edit()
            .putString(PREF_RESTORE, gameData)
            .commit();
    Log.d("UT3", "state = " + gameData);
}
```

Finally let's change the reportWinner() method to play a little jingle when the game is over, depending on who won:

ticTacToev4/src/main/java/org/example/tictactoe/GameActivity.java

```
public void reportWinner(final Tile.Owner winner) {
    AlertDialog.Builder builder = new AlertDialog.Builder(this);
    if (mMediaPlayer != null && mMediaPlayer.isPlaying()) {
        mMediaPlayer.stop();
        mMediaPlayer.reset();
        mMediaPlayer.release();
    }
    builder.setMessage(getString(R.string.declare_winner, winner));
    builder.setCancelable(false);
    builder.setPositiveButton(R.string.ok_label,
            new DialogInterface.OnClickListener() {
                @Override
                public void onClick(DialogInterface dialogInterface, int i) {
                    finish();
                }
            });
    final Dialog dialog = builder.create();
    mHandler.postDelayed(new Runnable() {
        @Override
        public void run() {
            mMediaPlayer = MediaPlayer.create(GameActivity.this,
                    winner == Tile.Owner.X ? R.raw.oldedgar_winner
                            : winner == Tile.Owner.O ? R.raw.notr_loser
                            : R.raw.department64_draw
            );
            mMediaPlayer.start();
            dialog.show();
        }
    }, 500);

    mGameFragment.initGame();  // Reset the board to the initial position
}
```

If there's music currently playing, we stop it with the MediaPlayer.stop() method. Then we set up a handler to run a piece of code after a delay of half a second (500ms). This code creates a new player, passing it the id of the sound to play. I picked three other clips from the freesound.org site for this purpose.

It Goes Ding When There's Stuff

When you're watching a TV show or movie, and something happens on screen that makes a noise, often the noise isn't recorded as it happens. To make it sound better, it's added in later during editing by the Foley artists. They put in all the clicks, whirs, footsteps, bangs, crashes, and thousands of other sounds during the feature. If they do their job right, you'll never know they were there. So sit through the credits next time, and look for the Foley.

In this example you're going to be the Foley artist by adding sound effects to the Tic-Tac-Toe game. In particular we want the game to make a noise when the user selects a tile on the board or presses the button to reset the game pieces. For these sounds we're going to use a different class better suited for short sound clips called SoundPool. Unlike MediaPlayer, a SoundPool can play multiple sounds at once. It keeps track of all the sounds and mixes them together.

We create a new SoundPool with the new SoundPool() constructor. Starting in Android 5.0 (Lollipop) we could use the SoundPool.Builder class, but since we want our app to run on earlier versions of Android, we need to use the old way. If the compiler gives you a warning message about this being deprecated, just ignore it. Don't worry; it will still work.

```
ticTacToev4/src/main/java/org/example/tictactoe/GameFragment.java
import android.media.AudioManager;
import android.media.SoundPool;

public class GameFragment extends Fragment {
    private int mSoundX, mSoundO, mSoundMiss, mSoundRewind;
    private SoundPool mSoundPool;
    private float mVolume = 1f;
    // ...
    @Override
    public void onCreate(Bundle savedInstanceState) {
        super.onCreate(savedInstanceState);
        // Retain this fragment across configuration changes.
        setRetainInstance(true);
        initGame();
        mSoundPool = new SoundPool(3, AudioManager.STREAM_MUSIC, 0);
        mSoundX = mSoundPool.load(getActivity(), R.raw.sergenious_movex, 1);
        mSoundO = mSoundPool.load(getActivity(), R.raw.sergenious_moveo, 1);
```

```
        mSoundMiss = mSoundPool.load(getActivity(), R.raw.erkanozan_miss, 1);
        mSoundRewind = mSoundPool.load(getActivity(), R.raw.joanne_rewind, 1);
    }
```

The SoundPool.load() method takes three parameters and returns the sound id of the loaded sound. The parameters are the current activity, the resource id of the raw sound file, and the priority of the sound.

This doesn't actually play anything—for that we call the SoundPool.play() method. Modify the click listener for each small tile (the code that's run when the tile is pressed) as follows:

ticTacToev4/src/main/java/org/example/tictactoe/GameFragment.java
```java
private void initViews(View rootView) {
        // ...
        inner.setOnClickListener(new View.OnClickListener() {
          @Override
          public void onClick(View view) {
            if (isAvailable(smallTile)) {
                mSoundPool.play(mSoundX, mVolume, mVolume, 1, 0, 1f);
                makeMove(fLarge, fSmall);
                think();
            } else {
                mSoundPool.play(mSoundMiss, mVolume, mVolume, 1, 0, 1f);
            }
          }
        });
        // ...
}
private void think() {
            // ...
            switchTurns();
            mSoundPool.play(mSoundO, mVolume, mVolume, 1, 0, 1f);
            makeMove(move[0], move[1]);
            switchTurns();
            // ...
}
```

First we play the X sound to indicate the user has moved. Then a second later we play the O sound to indicate the computer has moved. If the user selected a tile that wasn't a valid move, we play a different sound to indicate the user missed pressing the right tile.

After making these changes, be sure to test them out by playing a game and making all the different sounds happen.

By the way, SoundPool.play() is quite a versatile method. It takes the following six parameters:

soundID
> a soundID returned by the load() function

leftVolume
> left volume value (range = 0.0 to 1.0)

rightVolume
> volume value (range = 0.0 to 1.0)

priority
> stream priority (0 = lowest priority)

loop
> loop mode (0 = no loop, -1 = loop forever)

rate
> playback rate (1.0 = normal playback, range 0.5 to 2.0)

Try playing around with the parameters to get different effects.

Fast-Forward >>

In this chapter, we covered playing audio clips using the Android SDK. We didn't discuss recording because most programs won't need to do that, but if you happen to be the exception, then look up the MediaRecorder class in the online documentation.[5]

In Chapter 7, *Adding Animation*, on page 101, we'll close out the Tic-Tac-Toe example by learning some simple animation techniques that can make a big difference in the enjoyment of your Android programs. If you don't need to do that right now, then you can skip ahead to Chapter 8, *Write Once, Test Everywhere*, on page 113 and learn about making your apps run on a variety of devices.

---

5. http://d.android.com/reference/android/media/MediaRecorder.html

CHAPTER 7

Adding Animation

One way to make your Android application more interesting and entertaining is to add animation. When done tastefully, animation can help turn a ho-hum program into something exciting and vibrant.

Instead of having things appear abruptly on the screen, have them fly or bounce in. Instead of a static background, bring it to life with a little movement. This is especially needed for games that are supposed to be fun anyway. Don't overdo it, though—the animation should add to the experience, not distract from it.

In this chapter we'll add two animated elements to the Tic-Tac-Toe game. First we'll put a scrolling background underneath the main menu. Then we'll make the tiles bounce around when you touch them.

The Never-Ending Scroller

We want a background image to be displayed on the opening screen. It will pan slowly toward the upper-left corner of the display. No seams can be visible, and the animation has to be very smooth. The figure shows what it will look like.

If you stare at this long enough, it will start moving.

Adding the View

To accomplish this we're going to make a new type of view called ScrollingView and make it cover the entire screen behind the game selection menu. Edit res/layout/activity_main.xml and insert this block as the first child of the FrameLayout element:

ticTacToev5/src/main/res/layout/activity_main.xml

```
<org.example.tictactoe.ScrollingView
    android:id="@+id/main_background"
    android:layout_width="match_parent"
    android:layout_height="match_parent"
    app:scrollingDrawable="@drawable/xando_background" />
```

There are two important things about this code. First, instead of a standard Android view it references org.example.tictactoe.ScrollingView, which we'll define in a moment. The other thing is that it sets a property we haven't seen before. The app:scrollingDrawable property is a custom property that controls the image that will be scrolled.

Defining Custom Properties

Note the app: prefix. This is an XML namespace, which we need to define as a property of the FrameLayout tag. Add this attribute after the definition of xmlns:android:

```
xmlns:app="http://schemas.android.com/apk/res-auto"
```

The special namespace is a clue to Android that it should look in our resources directory for the definition of any properties that begin with "app:". Create a file called res/values/attrs_scrolling_view.xml that contains the following definition:

ticTacToev5/src/main/res/values/attrs_scrolling_view.xml

```
<resources>
    <declare-styleable name="ScrollingView">
        <attr name="scrollingDrawable" format="color|reference" />
    </declare-styleable>
</resources>
```

The name of the file isn't important as long as you put it in the right directory. This declares that ScrollingViews can have a single attribute named scrollingDrawable, which can be either a color or a reference to a drawable.

Background Information

The background we're going to scroll is a simple repeated bitmap:

ticTacToev5/src/main/res/drawable/xando_background.xml

```
<?xml version="1.0" encoding="utf-8"?>
<bitmap xmlns:android="http://schemas.android.com/apk/res/android"
    android:src="@drawable/xando"
    android:tileMode="repeat" />
```

This refers to a file called xando.png in the res/drawable-mdpi directory. You can use any image you like as long as it can be tiled seamlessly. (That's easier said than done.) You can also find many examples on the web, but I created one by hand in a paint program, which you can download from the ticTacToev5 example on the book's website.[1]

Slip-Sliding in the Rain

Now all that's left to do is to create the scrolling view. Let's start with an outline of the class:

ticTacToev5/src/main/java/org/example/tictactoe/ScrollingView.java
```java
package org.example.tictactoe;

import android.content.Context;
import android.content.res.TypedArray;
import android.graphics.Canvas;
import android.graphics.drawable.Drawable;
import android.util.AttributeSet;
import android.view.View;

/**
 * This custom view draws a background image that scrolls indefinitely.
 */
public class ScrollingView extends View {
  private Drawable mBackground;
  private int mScrollPos;
}
```

Android requires that we add these constructors for custom views that take attributes:

ticTacToev5/src/main/java/org/example/tictactoe/ScrollingView.java
```java
public ScrollingView(Context context) {
  super(context);
  init(null, 0);
}

public ScrollingView(Context context, AttributeSet attrs) {
  super(context, attrs);
  init(attrs, 0);
}

public ScrollingView(Context context, AttributeSet attrs, int defStyle) {
  super(context, attrs, defStyle);
  init(attrs, defStyle);
}
```

The init() method, shown on the next page, finds the attribute list and picks out the one we want:

---

1. http://pragprog.com/book/eband4

ticTacToev5/src/main/java/org/example/tictactoe/ScrollingView.java

```java
private void init(AttributeSet attrs, int defStyle) {
   // Load custom view attributes
   final TypedArray a = getContext().obtainStyledAttributes(
         attrs, R.styleable.ScrollingView, defStyle, 0);

   // Get background
   if (a.hasValue(R.styleable.ScrollingView_scrollingDrawable)) {
      mBackground = a.getDrawable(
            R.styleable.ScrollingView_scrollingDrawable);
      mBackground.setCallback(this);
   }

   // Done with attributes
   a.recycle();
}
```

The actual work is done by the onDraw() method:

ticTacToev5/src/main/java/org/example/tictactoe/ScrollingView.java

```java
@Override
protected void onDraw(Canvas canvas) {
   super.onDraw(canvas);

   // See how big the view is (ignoring padding)
   int contentWidth = getWidth();
   int contentHeight = getHeight();

   // Draw the background
   if (mBackground != null) {
      // Make the background bigger than it needs to be
      int max = Math.max(mBackground.getIntrinsicHeight(),
            mBackground.getIntrinsicWidth());
      mBackground.setBounds(0, 0, contentWidth * 4, contentHeight * 4);

      // Shift where the image will be drawn
      mScrollPos += 2;
      if (mScrollPos >= max) mScrollPos -= max;
      setTranslationX(-mScrollPos);
      setTranslationY(-mScrollPos);

      // Draw it and indicate it should be drawn next time too
      mBackground.draw(canvas);
      this.invalidate();
   }
}
```

The important part of this method is the mBackground.draw() call, which draws the background Xs and Os on the screen. They appear to move because of the calls to setTranslationX() and setTranslationY() immediately before drawing.

onDraw() will be called over and over, once per frame, because of the invalidate() call at the end. And each time it is called, the scroll position (mScrollPos) is incremented by 2 so the x and y positions slowly crawl to the upper left. Any seams are hidden by making the background bigger so you never see the edge.

Bouncing Tiles

In the game screen, having Xs and Os appear out of nowhere isn't realistic, so let's make the tiles appear more lifelike. We'll make them splat onto the grid as if they were made of jelly.

Principles of Animation

In 1981, Disney animators Ollie Johnston and Frank Thomas published a famous book called *The Illusion of Life: Disney Animation [JT95]*, which explained the animation process used by animators since the 1930s. In the book they outlined twelve basic principles of animation,[2] which are still in use to this day.

The principles are essential to all animation, not just comics, so I'm going to list them here and then show how to apply some of them using Android calls. See the online reference for a full description:

1. Squash and stretch
2. Anticipation
3. Staging
4. Straight ahead action and pose to pose
5. Follow through and overlapping action
6. Slow in and slow out
7. Arc
8. Secondary action
9. Timing
10. Exaggeration
11. Solid drawing
12. Appeal

In Android, animation is defined in (what else?) XML files. Create a new directory in the res directory called animator and a new file called tictactoe.xml containing the following:

---

2.   http://en.wikipedia.org/wiki/12_basic_principles_of_animation

ticTacToev5/src/main/res/animator/tictactoe.xml
```xml
<?xml version="1.0" encoding="utf-8"?>
<set xmlns:android="http://schemas.android.com/apk/res/android">
    <objectAnimator
        android:duration="500"
        android:interpolator="@android:interpolator/overshoot"
        android:propertyName="scaleX"
        android:valueFrom="2"
        android:valueTo="1" />
    <objectAnimator
        android:duration="700"
        android:interpolator="@android:interpolator/overshoot"
        android:propertyName="scaleY"
        android:valueFrom="2"
        android:valueTo="1" />

</set>
```

This defines an animation set, which is an animation that affects two or more arbitrary properties of an object at the same time. In this case, the properties being animated are the scale (size) of the object in both the X (width) and Y (height) directions.

For both properties we start out with an exaggerated size of two times the normal size (principle #10), and then start making it smaller until it reaches the normal size. We just define the starting and ending poses and let the computer fill in the rest (#4).

The timing of the animation (#9) is set by the duration property. Note that the two durations are slightly different, creating a squash and stretch effect (#1). The intermediate positions are controlled by the interpolator property, which we use to achieve a follow-through or overshoot effect (#5). With different settings, interpolators can also be used to simulate slow in and slow out (#6), anticipation (#2) and arcs (#7).

Step Right Up

Now that we've defined a generic animation, we need to apply it to the tile(s) at the appropriate time. In GameFragment.java add a call to animate() at the top of the addAvailable() method:

ticTacToev5/src/main/java/org/example/tictactoe/GameFragment.java
```java
private void addAvailable(Tile tile) {
    tile.animate();
    mAvailable.add(tile);
}
```

That will cause newly available tiles to perform the bouncing animation.

Next add another animate() call as the first line of the onClick() method inside initViews():

ticTacToev5/src/main/java/org/example/tictactoe/GameFragment.java
```
public void onClick(View view) {
   smallTile.animate();
   // ...
}
```

That will cause each tile the user touches to bounce.

Finally, add a call in the makeMove() method right here:

ticTacToev5/src/main/java/org/example/tictactoe/GameFragment.java
```
if (winner != oldWinner) {
   largeTile.animate();
   largeTile.setOwner(winner);
}
```

This will cause the large board to animate when either X or O wins it. See the example code on the book's website if you have trouble finding the right places.

Now let's add the animate() method that we just called.

Watch the Bouncing Tile

After all that setup, there's not much left to do to make the animation actually run. First we need to add a couple of import statements near the top of Tile.java:

ticTacToev5/src/main/java/org/example/tictactoe/Tile.java
```
import android.animation.Animator;
import android.animation.AnimatorInflater;
```

And here's the definition of the animate() method itself:

ticTacToev5/src/main/java/org/example/tictactoe/Tile.java
```
public void animate() {
   Animator anim = AnimatorInflater.loadAnimator(mGame.getActivity(),
         R.animator.tictactoe);
   if (getView() != null) {
      anim.setTarget(getView());
      anim.start();
   }
}
```

The first line loads the tictactoe.xml animation that we defined earlier. Then if a view is associated with this tile, we set that as the target of the animation and start it.

That's all there is to running an animation!

The Story So Far

Congratulations! Except for some tweaks in the next chapter, we're done with the Tic-Tac-Toe example. By creating this sample program, you've learned everything you need to know to build basic Android applications. This includes the following:

- Creating apps using activities and fragments
- Building user interfaces with XML
- Responding to user input
- Adding sound and animations

The following figure shows the finished product.

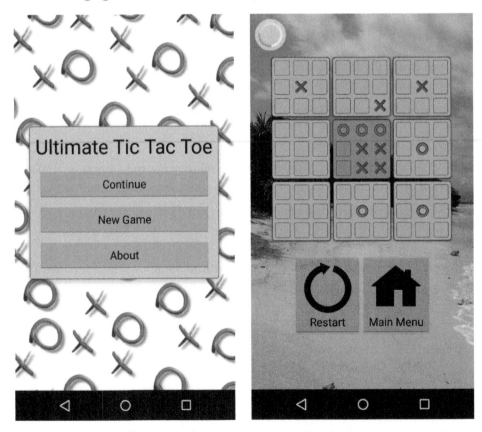

Take a break and give the game a try. Show it off to your friends, and then start hacking on it to improve it. Remember that the complete source code for this and all examples can be found on the book's website.

Fast-Forward >>

In this chapter we added two animations to the Tic-Tac-Toe game: a scrolling background for the main screen, and bouncing tiles in the game screen. The techniques you learned will be useful in a number of situations.

In the next chapter we'll explore how to make our apps compatible with a wide variety of screen sizes and devices. We'll fix up our game to look good and work well with both phones and tablets. In Chapter 9, *Publishing to the Play Store*, on page 125 we'll look at publishing an app to the Google Play Store. Then starting in Chapter 10, *Connecting to the World*, on page 137 we'll move on to more advanced topics such as accessing the Internet and using location-based services.

Part III

Thinking Outside the Box

CHAPTER 8

Write Once, Test Everywhere

Today, Android can be found in a bewildering array of mobile phones, tablets, watches, TVs, and other devices. This is both a blessing and a curse. It's a blessing for consumers because they can choose between Android-powered devices of different shapes, sizes, and prices. But for developers, it can be a curse to try to support all those variations.

To complicate things, the rapid pace of Android development has left a fragmented trail of devices running different versions of the platform in its wake. The following lists all the versions of Android ever released. See the Android Platform Dashboard[1] for an up-to-date chart showing the percentage of devices running each version of Android.

Versions marked with an asterisk (*) are no longer in use.

Android version codes and API levels are specified in the Build.VERSION_CODES class.

Version	Code name	API	Released	Comments
1.0*	BASE	1	Sep 2008	First version
1.1*	BASE_1_1	2	Feb 2009	Attachments, Marquee
1.5*	CUPCAKE	3	May 2009	Widgets, Virtual keyboards
1.6*	DONUT	4	Sep 2009	High- and low-density displays
2.0*	ECLAIR	5	Nov 2009	Exchange accounts
2.0.1*	ECLAIR_0_1	6	Dec 2009	Multi-touch
2.1*	ECLAIR_MR1	7	Jan 2010	Live wallpaper
2.2*	FROYO	8	May 2010	SD card installs
2.3*	GINGERBREAD	9	Dec 2010	Native gaming

---

1.   http://d.android.com/resources/dashboard/platform-versions.html

Version	Code name	API	Released	Comments
2.3.3	GINGERBREAD_MR1	10	Feb 2011	NFC
3.0*	HONEYCOMB	11	Feb 2011	Fragments, ActionBars, Holo theme
3.1*	HONEYCOMB_MR1	12	May 2011	USB API, Joysticks
3.2*	HONEYCOMB_MR2	13	June 2011	7" screens
4.0*	ICE_CREAM_SAND-WICH	14	Oct 2011	Roboto, Unified phone/tablet UI
4.0.3	ICE_CREAM_SAND-WICH_MR1	15	Dec 2011	Social stream API
4.1	JELLY_BEAN	16	Jun 2012	Project Butter, systrace, Expandable notifications
4.2	JELLY_BEAN_MR1	17	Nov 2012	Multi-user, wireless display
4.3	JELLY_BEAN_MR2	18	Jul 2013	OpenGL ES 3.0, SELinux, Restricted profiles
4.4	KITKAT	19	Oct 2013	Chromium WebView, Immersive mode
4.4W*	KITKAT_WATCH	20	Jun 2014	Android Wear
5.0	LOLLIPOP	21	Oct 2014	ART, Material design, Project Volta
5.1	LOLLIPOP MR1	22	Mar 2015	Multiple SIM cards, Carrier services

This chapter will cover how to support multiple Android versions and screen resolutions in one program. The first step is testing.

Gentlemen, Start Your Emulators

For most of this book I've been telling you to target your applications to version 4.1 of the Android platform (also known as Jelly Bean). However, there's one little problem with this advice: your programs may not actually run on those older versions. The only reliable way of telling whether it will work is to test it. And short of buying one of every Android phone and tablet on the market, the best way to test your program on different Android versions and screen sizes is to try it in the emulator. To do this, you'll need to set up several virtual devices with different versions and sizes.

Emulators "R" Us

Including the Nexus 5 AVD created for you in *Running on the Android Emulator*, on page 9, I recommend that you create the following virtual devices for testing:

Name	Target	Resolution	Density
Nexus 4	4.1	768×1280	xhdpi (extra-high dots per inch)
Nexus 5	5.1	1080×1920	xxhdpi (extra-extra high)
Nexus 7	4.2	1200×1920	xhdpi
Nexus 9	4.4	2048×1536	xhdpi

Note: As new versions of Android come out, be sure to include them in your testing matrix. Consult the Android Platform Dashboard to decide which older versions you can eliminate.

Try it now by creating the Nexus 4 emulator running Android 4.2. Click the AVD Manager button in Android Studio to start the AVD Manager, as shown in the following figure.

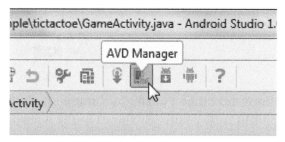

Click the Create Virtual Device... button, and then select Nexus 4 from the Phone category. Select Next to continue:.

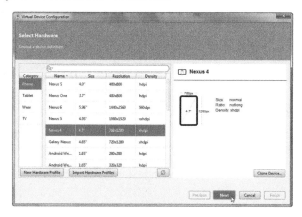

Now select a system image (see the following figure). We want the Nexus 4 to run version 4.1 (Jelly Bean) so select the x86 version for that release. (You always want to use the Intel x86 emulator if you can because it is several times faster than the ARM emulator, even though most real devices use ARM processors.)

If the image isn't already downloaded, click the Download link to get it first.

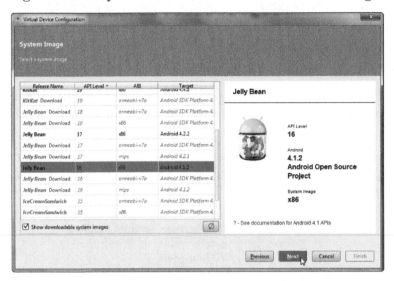

Click Next to continue, and then Finish. Continue with all the other versions listed in the table until you see the list shown in the following figure.

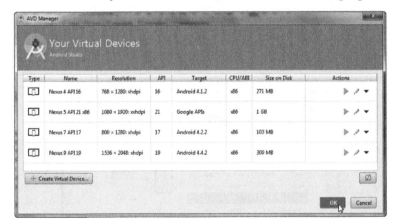

Testing Strategy

You can use the Nexus 5 AVD for development and then test your program in the other AVDs before you release the application. And don't forget to try it in both portrait and landscape modes. (In the emulator, press `Ctrl+F11` or use the `7` or `9` keys on the keypad (NumLock off) to toggle between portrait and landscape.)

Unless you have a very powerful desktop computer, you probably won't be able to run all these AVDs at once. In practice, I find that running only one at a time works best.

Close down the Nexus 5 emulator if you're currently running it and start the Nexus 4 one. In the AVD Manager, click the Play icon in the Actions column. Wait until the emulator comes up to the home screen, and turn off the screen lock if it appears. Now let's see some of the things that can go wrong.

The Good, The Bad,...

Run the Tic-Tac-Toe program now and it should appear in the Nexus 4 emulator. Unfortunately it doesn't look very good, as you can see in the figure. (Wipe that grin off your face.)

Start a game by pressing the New Game button; everything looks fine until we make a move. Then all the empty squares go black, as the figure shows.

So how do you fix problems like this?

One technique you can use is to try it on newer and newer versions of Android until you find one that works. If you do that, you'll see that the smearing problem goes away with Android 4.3 and the black squares are fixed in version 4.2. You could use that knowledge to go back into the release notes for both versions to see what changed, or even examine the source code. That would take a while.

Another approach, which is less scientific but often produces quick results, is to try to reimplement the code in a different way and see if it works better. I call this the "Fonzie" method after the character Fonzie in "Happy Days." In the show, the jukebox was always breaking down, and Fonzie would walk up and give it a little kick or bump to get it working again. Likewise, you can make little modifications in the code to see what effect that has on the problem.

In this case, I used a combination of both methods to fix the problems. First I found the versions where the problems went away, but there was no obvious cause for the change in the release notes. So then I started modifying the code. With a little tweaking I discovered that if you change this code in ScrollingView.java:

ticTacToev5/src/main/java/org/example/tictactoe/ScrollingView.java

```
// Shift where the image will be drawn
mScrollPos += 2;
if (mScrollPos >= max) mScrollPos -= max;
setTranslationX(-mScrollPos);
setTranslationY(-mScrollPos);
```

to this:

ticTacToev6/src/main/java/org/example/tictactoe/ScrollingView.java

```
// Shift where the image will be drawn
mScrollPos += 2;
if (mScrollPos >= max) mScrollPos -= max;
canvas.translate(-mScrollPos, -mScrollPos);
```

it fixes the smearing problem. Then looking at the definition of tile_empty.xml:

ticTacToev5/src/main/res/drawable/tile_empty.xml
```
<shape xmlns:android="http://schemas.android.com/apk/res/android"
       android:shape="rectangle">
  <stroke
      android:width="@dimen/stroke_width"
      android:color="@color/dark_border_color"/>
  <corners android:radius="@dimen/corner_radius"/>
</shape>
```

I found that adding a solid color in the shape like this:

ticTacToev6/src/main/res/drawable/tile_empty.xml
```
<solid android:color="@color/gray_color"/>
```

fixes the black square problem.

If Nothing Else Works

For tough problems, you can use version tests. For example, you could disable the scrolling effect completely by adding code that checks for a recent version of Android:

```
// Avoid running code that doesn't work on older versions
if (Build.VERSION.SDK_INT >= Build.VERSION_CODES.KITKAT) {
    // Scrolling code goes here...
}
```

For resource files, you can use different resources for different versions of Android. We'll explore this more in the next section.

Finally, if there's no easy way to make it work, you can update the minimum target version for your application. Keep in mind, however, doing so will limit your audience.

All Screens Great and Small

Supporting different screen sizes, resolutions, and pixel densities is important because you want your application to look its best on as many Android devices as possible. Android will try to scale your user interface to fit the device, but it doesn't always do a great job of it. The only way to tell is through, you guessed it, testing. Use the emulator types recommended in *Gentlemen, Start Your Emulators*, on page 114 to make sure your program works on the most common sizes.

As a test, try running the Tic-Tac-Toe program in the Nexus 9 emulator. You'll find that the menu on the main activity and the board in the game activity look too small. That's because all the sizes are specified in dps, but the tablet has a much larger physical screen than the phone (that is, more dps across and down). So we need to increase the size on tablets.

> ### Google Wear, TV, and Auto
>
> It's possible to run the same program on watches (Google Wear), televisions (Google TV), and automobiles (Google Auto) that you run on phones and tablets. The first step is to try them out in the emulator to see how they look, and then adjust the layouts and dimensions. Most of these devices don't support touchscreens, so your app will have to be modified to use alternate input methods.
>
> For Wear apps you have two choices: running directly on the watch, or running on a phone and displaying notifications on the watch. To learn more about Wear apps, see the Building Apps for Wearables[a] training on the Google website.
>
> TV apps should be specially designed for the "lean-back" experience because the screen is typically several feet from the user. The Building Apps for TV[b] training contains a number of helpful tips.
>
> Automobiles are a new growth opportunity for Android. To learn more about that, see the Building Apps for Auto[c] section of the online doc.
>
> ---
>
> a.   http://d.android.com/training/building-wearables.html
> b.   http://d.android.com/training/tv
> c.   http://d.android.com/training/auto

Specifying Alternate Resources

To tweak the layouts or images for particular configurations of Android devices, you use suffixes in the resource directory names.

For example, you can put images for extra-high-density displays in the res/drawable-xhdpi directory, high-density displays in res/drawable-hdpi, and medium-density displays in res/drawable-mdpi. All the examples do that for their program icons, which will be shown on the home screen. Graphics that are density-independent (that shouldn't be scaled) go in the res/drawable-nodpi directory.

Luckily we've placed all our sizes in one place: dimens.xml in the values directory. So all we need to do is create different versions of that file and place them in directories qualified by different sizes of screens. These will show up in the Project view as either directories (in Project mode) or with labels next to them indicating the qualifier used (in Android mode).

The following is a list of the valid directory name qualifiers, in order of precedence (see the online documentation[2] for a full explanation of how Android finds the best matching directory):

Qualifier	Values
MCC and MNC	Mobile country code and optional mobile network code. I don't recommend using this.
Language and region	Two-letter language and optional two-letter region code (preceded by lowercase r). For example: fr, en-rUS, fr-rFR, es-rES.
Layout direction	Layout direction of your application. This should be ldltr for left to right (the default), or ldrtl for right to left.
Smallest width	The shortest dimension of the available screen size. For example: sw320dp, sw600dp, sw720dp.
Available width	Minimum available screen width in dp units at which the resource should be used. For example: w720dp, w1024dp.
Available height	Minimum available screen height in dp units at which the resource should be used. For example, h720dp, h1024dp.
Screen dimensions	small, normal, large, xlarge.
Wider/taller screens	long, notlong.
Screen orientation	port, land.
UI mode	car, desk, television, appliance, watch.
Night mode	night, notnight.
Screen pixel density	ldpi, mdpi, hdpi, xhdpi, xxhdpi, xxxhdpi, nodpi, tvpi.
Touchscreen type	notouch, finger.
Keyboard available?	keysexposed, keyshidden, keyssoft.
Keyboard type	nokeys, qwerty, 12key.
Navigation available?	navexposed, navhidden.
Navigation type	nonav, dpad, trackball, wheel.
SDK version	API level supported by the device (preceded by lowercase "v"). For example: v16, v21.

To use more than one qualifier, just string them together with a hyphen (-) in between. For example, the res/drawable-fr-land-hdpi directory could contain pictures for high-density displays in landscape mode in French. Ordering is important.

Resizing the Game

For our Tic-Tac-Toe example, let's look at the files you need to create.

The base settings in values/dimens.xml will be used for the smallest phones. Right-click on the res directory and select New > Directory to create four additional directories: values-sw360dp, -sw600dp, -sw720dp, and -w820dp (note we

---

2. http://d.android.com/guide/topics/resources/providing-resources.html#BestMatch

use "smallest width" for all but the last one, and the last one may already exist). The directories won't appear in the Project view in Android mode, but you'll be prompted for the qualifier when you try to put a new file there. In each directory, put a new dimens.xml file that overrides just the values you want to change. Here are the ones I used:

values-sw360dp (phones):

```
ticTacToev6/src/main/res/values-sw360dp/dimens.xml
<resources>
    <dimen name="tile_size">35dp</dimen>
</resources>
```

values-sw600dp (small tablets):

```
ticTacToev6/src/main/res/values-sw600dp/dimens.xml
<resources>
    <!-- Default screen margins, per the Android Design guidelines. -->
    <dimen name="activity_horizontal_margin">16dp</dimen>
    <dimen name="activity_vertical_margin">16dp</dimen>

    <dimen name="tile_size">50dp</dimen>
    <dimen name="tile_padding">5dp</dimen>
    <dimen name="small_board_padding">4dp</dimen>
    <dimen name="small_board_margin">4dp</dimen>
</resources>
```

values-sw720dp (medium tablets):

```
ticTacToev6/src/main/res/values-sw720dp/dimens.xml
<resources>
    <dimen name="tile_size">70dp</dimen>
</resources>
```

values-w820dp (wide screens):

```
ticTacToev6/src/main/res/values-w820dp/dimens.xml
<resources>
    <dimen name="activity_horizontal_margin">64dp</dimen>
</resources>
```

Finding the right values requires a bit of trial and error. Luckily Android Studio has a feature that makes it easier.

This Preview Approved for Any Audience

Using Android Studio's Preview window lets you see how changes affect several screen sizes at once. Simply edit a layout file such as res/layout/activity_game.xml, make your window as large as you can, and select the Configuration icon in the Preview window, which appears to the right of the XML. If you don't see a Preview window, you can open it with the View > Tool Windows > Preview menu command. Select Preview All Screen Sizes to see several types of phones and tablets side by side in landscape and portrait modes, as shown in the following figure.

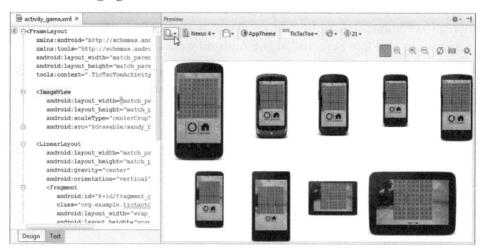

Then create and edit your dimens.xml files, coming back to the activity_game.xml preview after each change. Repeat until it looks good on all the screens. As a final test, try out the game on each of your emulators and on a real device. Be sure to rotate the screen to test both orientations.

Going Out with Style

Our program needs one more tweak. Android 5.0 (Lollipop) introduced a new "material" theme that changes the way certain UI elements appear and behave. When running on Android 5 and above, we want to use the latest look and feel; otherwise the app will look dated. To do this, create a res/values-v21 directory containing a new styles.xml (21 is the API level for Android 5.0):

ticTacToev6/src/main/res/values-v21/styles.xml
```xml
<?xml version="1.0" encoding="utf-8"?>
<resources>
    <!-- Base application theme. -->
    <style name="AppTheme"
           parent="android:Theme.Material.Light.NoActionBar.Fullscreen">
    </style>
</resources>
```

This overrides the style for the application to use the Material theme for full-screen apps. You can see the difference by going to the Preview window and selecting Preview Android Versions from the configurations drop-down menu.

Fast-Forward >>

Supporting multiple versions of Android running on multiple hardware devices with multiple screen sizes isn't easy. In this chapter, we've covered the most common issues and solutions to get you started. If you find yourself wanting more, I recommend reading the excellent best-practices document called "Supporting Multiple Screens" at the Android website.[3]

You've worked hard to get your application to this point. Now comes the fun part: letting other people use it. The next chapter will cover how to publish your app to the Google Play Store.

---

3. http://d.android.com/guide/practices/screens_support.html

CHAPTER 9

Publishing to the Play Store

Up to now you've just been creating software to run in the emulator or to download to your personal Android phone. Are you ready to take the next step? By publishing to the Google Play Store,[1] you can make your application available to millions of other Android users. This chapter will show you how.

Preparing

The first step of publishing an application to the Play Store is, well, to write the application. See the rest of the book for directions on how to do that. But simply writing code isn't enough. Your program needs to be of a high quality, free of bugs (yeah right), and compatible with as many devices as possible. Here are a few tips to help you:

- Test it on at least one real device before letting anyone else see it. If you forget all the other tips, remember this one.

- Keep your program simple, and polish the heck out of it. Make your program do one thing well, rather than a lot of things poorly.

- Pick a good Java package name, such as com.yourcompany.prog-name, that you can live with for a long time. Android uses the package name defined in AndroidManifest.xml as the primary identifier for your application. No two programs can have the same package name, and once you upload a program to the Play Store with that name, you can't change it without completely removing it, requiring all users to uninstall, and publishing a new program.

---

1. http://play.google.com/store

- Pick a meaningful value for android:versionCode= and android:versionName= in your AndroidManifest.xml file.[2] Consider future updates, and leave room for them in your naming scheme.

- Follow the Android best practices,[3] such as designing for performance, responsiveness, and seamlessness.

- Follow the user interface design guidelines,[4] such as icon design, menu design, and proper use of the Back button.

Compatibility with multiple devices is one of the toughest challenges facing the Android programmer. One issue you'll have to deal with is users having different screen sizes on their devices. See Chapter 8, *Write Once, Test Everywhere*, on page 113 for advice.

Although first impressions and compatibility are important, you'll need to strike a balance between tweaking and polishing your application to make it perfect versus releasing it in a timely fashion. Once you think it's ready, the next step is to sign it.

Signing

Android requires that all applications be packaged up into an .apk and signed with a digital certificate before it will consider running them. This is true for the emulator and for your personal testing devices, but it's especially true for programs that you want to publish on the Play Store.

"But wait," you say, "I haven't been packaging or signing anything up to now." Actually, you have. The Android SDK tools have been secretly building and signing everything using a certificate that Google created using a known alias and password. Because the password was known, you were never prompted for it and probably never even knew it existed. However, the debug certificate can't be used for applications in the Play Store, so now it's time to take off the training wheels and make your own certificate.

There are two ways to do it: by hand with the standard Java keytool and jarsigner commands[5] or automatically with Android Studio. I'm just going to cover the Android Studio way.

---

2. http://d.android.com/guide/publishing/versioning.html
3. http://d.android.com/guide/practices
4. http://d.android.com/design
5. http://d.android.com/tools/publishing/app-signing.html

From the menu at the top of the screen, select Build > Generate Signed APK.... Select the module you want to sign and click Next (see the following figure).

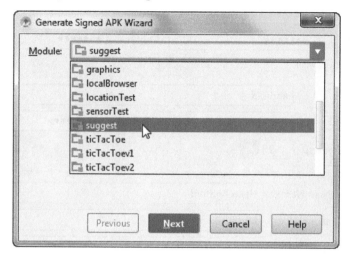

If this is your first time signing an application, then in the next screen click the "Create new..." button. You'll be prompted for the key store path and a bunch of other information needed to create your key store and the key it contains (see the figure on page 128).

Important: Write down and protect your passwords. If you forget them, it renders your keys useless and you won't be able to update your app.

You'll return to the previous screen with all the values filled in, as shown in the figure on page 129.

You should use the same key for all versions of all your applications and take the appropriate precautions for preventing your private key from falling into the wrong hands. Make a backup in Google Drive or some other safe location just in case.

Select Next and then Finish to start the signing process. Android Studio will display a message (see the following figure) when signing is complete.

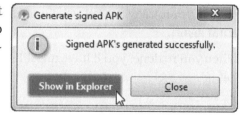

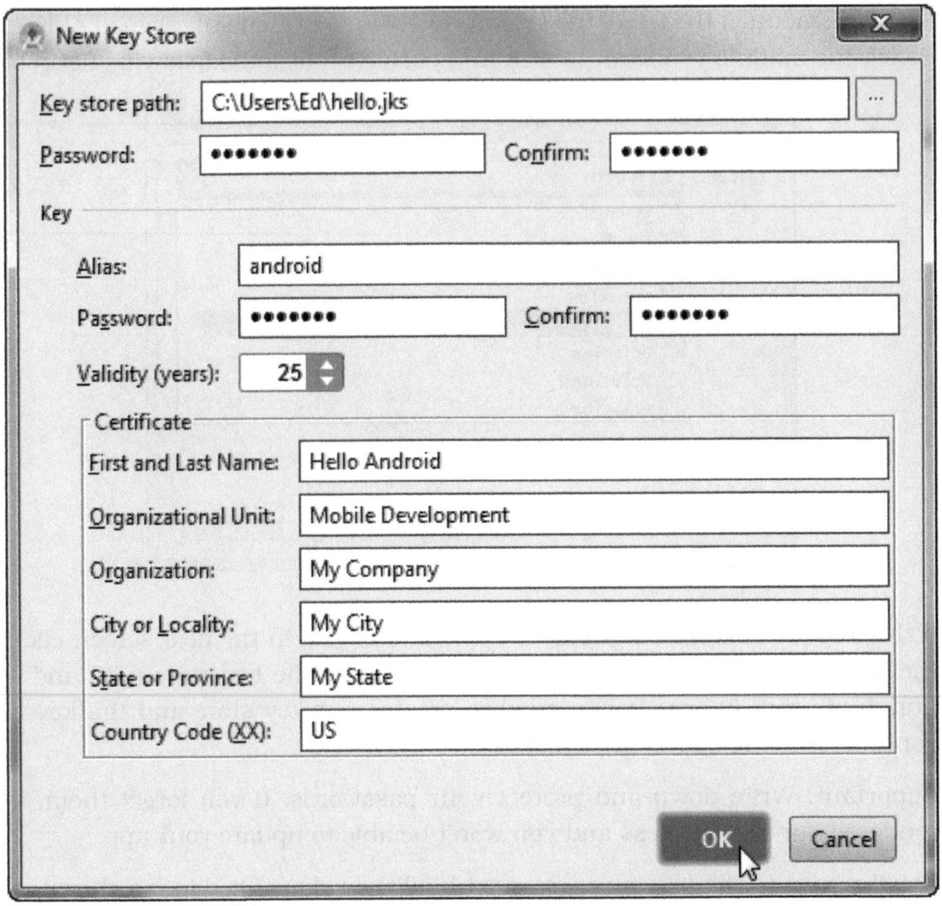

Figure 4—Whatever you do, don't forget your passwords.

Note: If you use the Google Maps API, then you'll need to get a new Maps API key from Google because it's tied to your digital certificate. Create a signed application once, obtain a new Maps API key using the online instructions,[6] change your AndroidManifest.xml file to use the new key, and then sign the program again.

When you're done, you'll have an APK file that's ready for testing and publishing.

---

6.   https://developers.google.com/maps/documentation/android

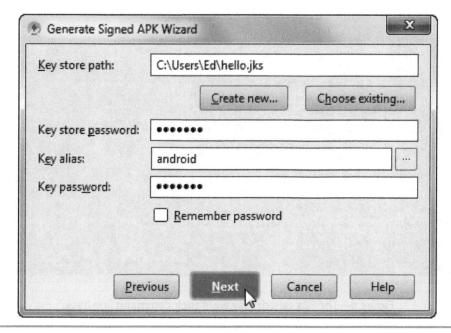

Figure 5—Don't lose this file.

Testing

Google recommends that you test your signed release version on at least one real device before publishing. (I confess that I rarely do this.) Getting the release version onto a device is a little more involved than the debug version.

Android Studio has a feature called "build variants" you can use to do it, but it doesn't work with the Signed APK Wizard. Instead, we'll use the command-line tools.

First, open a command window (sometimes called a shell or terminal window) and change your current directory to the location where the signed APK file was created. This is shown in the figure on page 130.

Plug in your device and run the adb devices command to make sure it can see it. Then run adb uninstall your.package.name to remove the debug version of your app from the device, replacing your.package.name with the name of your package defined in AndroidManifest.xml. Finally, run adb install app-release.apk, substituting the name of your APK file to copy the program onto your phone or tablet.

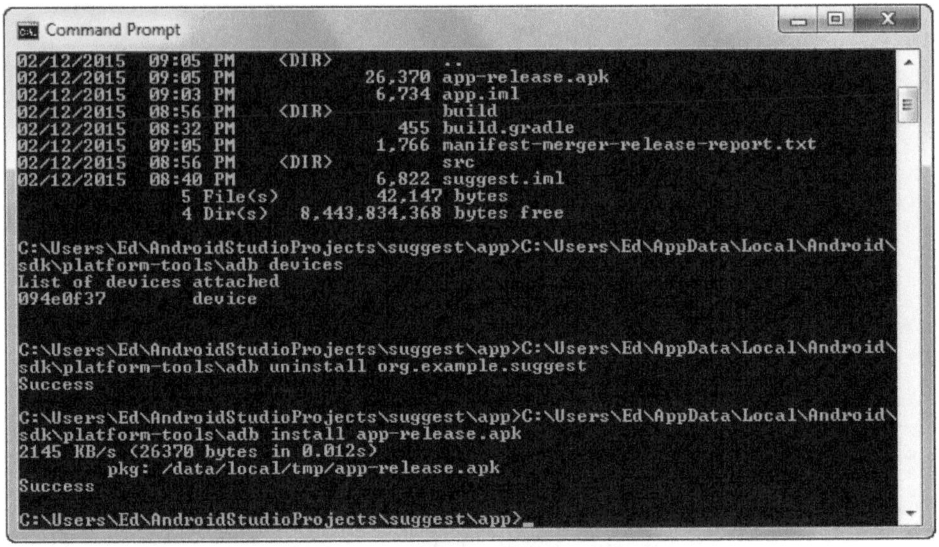

Figure 6—The 80s called; they want their command line back.

After you have the app copied, go to your device and locate the program in the apps list and tap on the icon to invoke it. Test it out to make sure it works correctly.

Publishing

The Google Play Store is a Google-hosted service you can use for posting all your programs. To get started with publishing, you first need to sign up as a registered developer on the Developer Console.[7] There's a small registration fee.

As an additional step, if you want to charge for your program, you'll need to sign up with a payment processor. The website will instruct you on how to do that.

Now you're ready to upload. Click the "Add new application" link, and fill out the form. Here are some tips:

- Unless you have a reason not to, set the Locations option to "All Current and Future Countries." New countries are being added all the time, and this way your application will be available to all of them.

---

7. http://play.google.com/apps/publish

- Do *not* supply your phone number in the application Contact Information. All Play Store users will be able to see this number, and they'll call it when they have problems. Of course, if you have a dedicated number and staff for phone support, then this tip doesn't apply.

Just to give you an example, here's how I filled out the form for the suggest example from *Using Web Services*, on page 155:

```
Upload new APK: (select Choose File and Upload)
Language: English
Title (English): Suggest
Short description (English):
  Web service example generates amazingly accurate search suggestions.
Description (English):
  Suggest matches a partial word or phrase you enter and comes
  up with a list of possible completions. Select one of the
  results to do a search on that item.

  The results are amazingly accurate, and are refined based on
  your location and searches other people are doing right now.

  This program is a sample from an upcoming edition of "Hello,
  Android" by Ed Burnette, published by the Pragmatic Programmers.
  It demonstrates calling web services, multi-threading, XML
  Parsing, and the Google Suggest API.

Application Type: Applications
Category: Libraries &amp; Demo

Content Rating: Everyone
Website: http://pragprog.com/book/eband4
Email: (my email address)
Phone: (blank)

Privacy Policy: (blank/not submitting a privacy policy)
Price: Free
Distribute in these countries: All
```

When you click the Publish button, your application will appear on the Google Play Store on all applicable devices. That's right; Google has only a minimal approval process, with a waiting period measured in hours, not weeks, and with no limits to what you can do in your programs. Well, almost. You still have to follow the Google Play Developer Program Policies.[8] Failure to adhere to the policies could result in your application being removed from the Google Play Store. Among other things, the guidelines say that your content must not be illegal, be obscene, promote hate or violence, or be unsuitable for

---

8. http://play.google.com/about/developer-content-policy.html

anyone younger than 18 years of age. In addition, it must not knowingly violate an authorized carrier's terms of service. There have been rare cases of programs being pulled because of user or carrier complaints, but as long as you use common sense, you shouldn't have anything to worry about.

The next section covers updates to already published applications.

Updating

Let's say your app has been in the Play Store for a little while and you want to make a change. The simplest kind of change is to the program's metadata—that is, the title, description, price, and all the other information you filled out in the previous section. To change this non-code information, simply select your program from the list on the Developer Console, make the change, and then click Submit Update.

Do you have a new version of your code? No problem, you can upload it from this page too. Before you do that, however, take a moment to verify that you've changed the two version numbers in your AndroidManifest.xml file. Increment android:versionCode= by one every time you upload (for example, from 1 to 2), and bump the human-readable version number in android:versionName= by the appropriate amount (for example, from 1.0.0 to 1.0.1 for a minor bug fix). Once the version number is correct and the package has been rebuilt and re-signed, select the APK section in the Developer Console, click the "Upload new APK" button, then click Browse, find your new .apk file, and click OK to send it to the server.

If possible, I suggest you perform occasional updates, keeping in mind these two conflicting observations:

- Frequent updates make users happy, because they think you're supporting them and listening to their suggestions.

- Frequent updates make users unhappy, because they're constantly bombarded by update notices and may uninstall apps that bother them too much.

Tips

Here are a few tips about the Play Store that I learned the hard way by publishing my own programs there:

- You can make a paid app free, but you can't make a free app paid. If there's any chance you might want to have a free (light) version and a paid (pro) version of your program, then create them both up front. Never take anything away that you put in the free version, or you risk a firestorm of protests.

• You won't be able to buy your own paid application using the same account under which you published it.

• Read all the comments left by users, but don't hesitate to report especially rude or vulgar ones as spam. Keep your comment area clean for useful feedback, both positive and negative.

• Don't get discouraged. People can be cruel, especially when posting anonymous comments. A thick skin and a sense of humor are invaluable tools of the trade.

• There are other markets besides the Google Play Store. By publishing to the Amazon Appstore[9] and other popular stores in addition to the Google Play Store you can reach more potential users.

Fast-Forward >>

You have all the tools you need to make successful Android applications and publish them on the Google Play Store. You could stop here, or you can continue reading about using Android's networking capabilities in Chapter 10, *Connecting to the World*, on page 137 and other services from Google in Chapter 12, *Using Google Play Services*, on page 169.

---

9. https://developer.amazon.com/appsandservices

Part IV

Beyond the Basics

Connecting to the World

Over the next few chapters, we'll cover more advanced topics such as network access and location-based services. You can write many useful applications without these features, but going beyond the basic features of Android will really help you add value to your programs, giving them much more functionality with a minimum of effort.

What do you use your mobile phone for? Aside from making calls, more and more people are using their phones as mobile Internet devices. Already, mobile phones and tablets have surpassed desktop computers as the number-one way to connect to the Internet.[1]

Android phones are well equipped for the connected world of the mobile Internet. First, Android provides a full-featured web browser based on the Chromium open source project.[2] This is the same browser technology that you'll find in Google Chrome for desktops. Chromium is a fork of WebKit,[3] which was also used in the Apple iPhone, iPad, and the Safari desktop browser.

Second, Android lets you embed the browser as a component right inside your application. Finally, Android gives your programs access to standard network services like TCP/IP sockets. This lets you consume web services from Google, Yahoo, Amazon, and many other sources on the Internet, including ones you write yourself.

In this chapter, you'll learn how to take advantage of Android's web browsing integration through three examples:

---

1. http://sewat.ch/2353616
2. http://www.chromium.org/Home
3. http://webkit.org

- *BrowserIntent*: Learn how to open an external web browser using an Android intent
- *BrowserView*: Find out how to embed a browser directly into your application
- *LocalBrowser*: Learn how JavaScript in an embedded WebView and Java code in your Android program can talk to each other

Chapter 11, *Calling Web Services*, on page 155 will cover using cloud-based services and resources from an Android program.

Browsing by Intent

The simplest thing you can do with Android's networking API is to open a browser on a web page of your choice. You might want to do this to provide a link to your home page from your program or to access some server-based application such as an ordering system. In Android all it takes is three lines of code plus a bit of setup.

To demonstrate, let's write a new example called BrowserIntent, which will have an edit field where you can enter a URL and a Go button you press to open the browser on that URL (see the figure). Start by creating a new "Hello, Android" project with the following values in the New Project wizard:

```
Application name: BrowserIntent
Company Domain: example.org
Form factors: Phone and Tablet
Minimum SDK: API 16: Android 4.1 (Jelly Bean)
Add activity: Blank Activity
Activity Name: MainActivity
Layout Name: activity_main
Title: Browser Intent
```

Once you have the basic program, change the layout file (res/layout/activity_main.xml) so it looks like this:

```
browserIntent/src/main/res/layout/activity_main.xml
<?xml version="1.0" encoding="utf-8"?>
<LinearLayout
    xmlns:android="http://schemas.android.com/apk/res/android"
    android:orientation="horizontal"
    android:layout_width="fill_parent"
    android:layout_height="fill_parent">
    <EditText
        android:id="@+id/url_field"
        android:layout_width="0dip"
        android:layout_height="wrap_content"
        android:layout_weight="1.0"
        android:lines="1"
        android:inputType="textUri"
        android:imeOptions="actionGo" />

    <Button
        android:id="@+id/go_button"
        android:layout_width="wrap_content"
        android:layout_height="wrap_content"
        android:text="@string/go_button" />
</LinearLayout>
```

This defines our two controls, an EditText control and a Button.

On EditText, we set android:layout_weight="1.0" to make the text area fill up all the horizontal space to the left of the button, and we also set android:lines="1" to limit the height of the control to one vertical line. Note that this has no effect on the amount of text the user can enter here, just the way it's displayed.

The options for android:inputType="textUri" and android:imeOptions="actionGo" are hints for how the soft keyboard should appear. They tell Android to replace the standard keyboard with one that has convenient buttons for entering web addresses. See the online documentation on the TextView[4] class for more information on input options.

As always, human-readable text should be put in a resource file, res/values/strings.xml.

```
browserIntent/src/main/res/values/strings.xml
<?xml version="1.0" encoding="utf-8"?>
<resources>
    <string name="app_name">BrowserIntent</string>
    <string name="action_settings">Settings</string>
    <string name="go_button">Go</string>
</resources>
```

---

4.   http://d.android.com/reference/android/widget/TextView.html

Next we need to fill in the onCreate() method in the MainActivity class. This is where we'll build the user interface and hook up all the behavior. If you don't feel like typing all this in, the complete source code is available online at the book's website.[5]

browserIntent/src/main/java/org/example/browserintent/MainActivity.java

```
Line 1   package org.example.browserintent;
  -
  -      import android.app.Activity;
  -      import android.content.Intent;
  5      import android.net.Uri;
  -      import android.os.Bundle;
  -      import android.view.KeyEvent;
  -      import android.view.View;
  -      import android.view.View.OnClickListener;
 10      import android.view.inputmethod.EditorInfo;
  -      import android.view.inputmethod.InputMethodManager;
  -      import android.widget.Button;
  -      import android.widget.EditText;
  -      import android.widget.TextView;
 15      import android.widget.TextView.OnEditorActionListener;
  -      public class MainActivity extends Activity {
  -          private EditText urlText;
  -          private Button goButton;
  -          @Override
 20          public void onCreate(Bundle savedInstanceState) {
  -              super.onCreate(savedInstanceState);
  -              setContentView(R.layout.activity_main);
  -              // Get a handle to all user interface elements
  -              urlText = (EditText) findViewById(R.id.url_field);
 25              goButton = (Button) findViewById(R.id.go_button);
  -              // Setup event handlers
  -              goButton.setOnClickListener(new OnClickListener() {
  -                  public void onClick(View view) {
  -                      openBrowser();
 30                  }
  -              });
  -              urlText.setOnEditorActionListener(new OnEditorActionListener() {
  -                  public boolean onEditorAction(TextView v, int actionId,
  -                      KeyEvent event) {
 35                  if (actionId == EditorInfo.IME_ACTION_GO) {
  -                      openBrowser();
  -                      InputMethodManager imm = (InputMethodManager)
  -                          getSystemService(INPUT_METHOD_SERVICE);
  -                      imm.hideSoftInputFromWindow(v.getWindowToken(), 0);
 40                      return true;
  -                  }
  -                  return false;
```

---

5. http://pragprog.com/book/eband4

```
  -           }
  -        });
45        }
  -  }
```

Inside onCreate(), we call setContentView() on line 22 to load the view from its definition in the layout resource, and then we call findViewById() on line 24 to get a handle to our two user interface controls.

Line 27 tells Android to run some code when the user selects the Go button, either by touching it or by navigating to it and pressing the center D-pad button. When that happens, we call the openBrowser() method, which will be defined in a moment.

If the user types an address and hits the Go button (or the Enter key if they have a physical keyboard), we also want the browser to open. To do this, we define a listener starting on line 32 that will be called when an action is performed on the edit field. If the Go button is pressed, then we call the openBrowser() method to open the browser; otherwise, we return false to let the edit control handle the event normally.

Now comes the part you've been waiting for: the openBrowser() method. As promised, it's three lines long:

browserIntent/src/main/java/org/example/browserintent/MainActivity.java
```java
/** Open a browser on the URL specified in the text box */
private void openBrowser() {
    Uri uri = Uri.parse(urlText.getText().toString());
    Intent intent = new Intent(Intent.ACTION_VIEW, uri);
    startActivity(intent);
}
```

The first line retrieves the address of the web page as a string (for example, "http://www.android.com") and converts it to a uniform resource identifier (URI).

Note: Don't leave off the "http://" part of the URL when you try this. If you do, the program will crash because Android won't know how to handle the address. In a real program you could add that if the user omitted it.

The next line creates a new Intent class with an action of ACTION_VIEW, passing it the Uri class just created as the object we want to view. Finally, we call the startActivity() method to request that this action be performed.

When the Browser activity starts, it will create its own view (see the following figure), and push your app into the background. If the user presses the Back button, the browser window will go away, and your application will resume.

But what if you want to see some of your user interface and a web page at the same time? Android allows you to do that by using the WebView class.

Web with a View

On your desktop computer, a web browser is a large, complicated, memory-gobbling program with all sorts of features like bookmarks, plug-ins, Flash animations, tabs, scroll bars, printing, and so forth.

When I was working on the Eclipse project and someone suggested replacing some common text views with embedded web browsers, I thought they were crazy. Wouldn't it make more sense, I argued, to simply enhance the text viewer to do italics or tables or whatever it was that was missing?

It turns out they weren't crazy because

- A web browser can be (relatively) lean and mean if you strip out everything but the basic rendering engine.
- If you enhance a text view to add more and more things that a browser engine can do, you end up with either an overly complicated, bloated text viewer or an underpowered browser.

Android provides a wrapper around the Chromium/WebKit browser engine called WebView that you can use to get the real power of a browser with very little overhead.

WebView works pretty much like any other Android view except that it has extra methods specific to the browser. We'll see how it works by doing an embedded version of the previous example. This one will be called BrowserView instead of BrowserIntent, since it uses an embedded View instead of an Intent. Start by creating a new "Hello, Android" project using these settings:

```
Application name: BrowserView
Company Domain: example.org
Form factors: Phone and Tablet
Minimum SDK: API 16: Android 4.1 (Jelly Bean)
Add activity: Blank Activity
Activity Name: MainActivity
Layout Name: activity_main
Title: Browser View
```

The layout file for BrowserView is similar to the one in BrowserIntent, except we've added a WebView at the bottom:

browserView/src/main/res/layout/activity_main.xml
```xml
<?xml version="1.0" encoding="utf-8"?>
<LinearLayout
    xmlns:android="http://schemas.android.com/apk/res/android"
    android:orientation="vertical"
    android:layout_width="fill_parent"
    android:layout_height="fill_parent">
    <LinearLayout
        android:orientation="horizontal"
        android:layout_width="fill_parent"
        android:layout_height="wrap_content">
        <EditText
            android:id="@+id/url_field"
            android:layout_width="0dip"
            android:layout_height="wrap_content"
            android:layout_weight="1.0"
            android:lines="1"
            android:inputType="textUri"
            android:imeOptions="actionGo" />
        <Button
            android:id="@+id/go_button"
            android:layout_width="wrap_content"
            android:layout_height="wrap_content"
            android:text="@string/go_button" />
    </LinearLayout>
    <WebView
        android:id="@+id/web_view"
        android:layout_width="fill_parent"
        android:layout_height="0dip"
        android:layout_weight="1.0" />
</LinearLayout>
```

We use two LinearLayout controls to make everything appear in the right place. The outermost control divides the screen into top and bottom regions; the top has the text area and button, and the bottom has the WebView. The innermost LinearLayout is the same as before; it just makes the text area go on the left and the button on the right.

The onCreate() method for BrowserView is exactly the same as before, except that now there's one extra view to look up:

browserView/src/main/java/org/example/browserview/MainActivity.java
```java
package org.example.browserview;
// ...
import android.webkit.WebView;
// ...

public class MainActivity extends Activity {
    private WebView webView;
    // ...
    @Override
    public void onCreate(Bundle savedInstanceState) {
        // ...
        webView = (WebView) findViewById(R.id.web_view);
        // ...
    }
}
```

The openBrowser() method, however, is different:

browserView/src/main/java/org/example/browserview/MainActivity.java
```java
/** Open a browser on the URL specified in the text box */
private void openBrowser() {
    webView.getSettings().setJavaScriptEnabled(true);
    webView.loadUrl(urlText.getText().toString());
}
```

The loadUrl() method causes the browser engine to begin loading and displaying a web page at the given address. It returns immediately even though the actual loading may take some time (if it finishes at all).

Don't forget to update the string resources:

browserView/src/main/res/values/strings.xml
```xml
<?xml version="1.0" encoding="utf-8"?>
<resources>
    <string name="app_name">BrowserView</string>
    <string name="action_settings">Settings</string>
    <string name="go_button">Go</string>
</resources>
```

We need to make one more change to the program. Add this line to AndroidMan-
ifest.xml before the <application> tag:

browserView/src/main/AndroidManifest.xml
```
<uses-permission android:name="android.permission.INTERNET" />
```

If you leave this out, Android will not give your application access to the
Internet, and you'll get a "Web page not available" error.

Joe asks:
Why Didn't BrowserIntent Need
<uses-permission>?

The previous example, BrowserIntent, simply fired off an intent to request that some
other application view the web page. That other application (the browser) is the one
that needs to ask for Internet permissions in its own AndroidManifest.xml.

Try running the program now, and enter a valid
web address starting with "http://"; when you
press Return or select the Go button, the web
page should appear (see the figure).

Depending on the address you entered, you may
have to supply the trailing "/" character because
we're not handling redirections.

WebView has dozens of other methods you can use
to control what is being displayed or get notifica-
tions on state changes. You can find a complete
list in the online documentation for WebView,[6] but
here are the methods you're most likely to need:

- addJavascriptInterface(): Allows a Java object to be
  accessed from JavaScript (more on this one
  in the next section)

- createSnapshot(): Creates a screenshot of the current page

- getSettings(): Returns a WebSettings object used to control the settings

- loadData(): Loads the given string data into the browser

- loadDataWithBaseURL(): Loads the given data using a base URL

---

6. http://d.android.com/reference/android/webkit/WebView.html

- loadUrl(): Loads a web page from the given URL

- setDownloadListener(): Registers callbacks for download events, such as when the user downloads a zip or APK file

- setWebChromeClient(): Registers callbacks for events that need to be done outside the WebView rectangle, such as updating the title or progress bar or opening a JavaScript dialog box

- setWebViewClient(): Lets the application set hooks in the browser to intercept events such as resource loads, key presses, and authorization requests

- stopLoading(): Stops the current page from loading

One of the most powerful things you can do with the WebView control is to talk back and forth between it and the Android application that contains it. Let's take a closer look at this feature now.

From JavaScript to Java and Back

Your Android device can do a number of cool things such as store local data, draw graphics, play music, make calls, and determine its location. Wouldn't it be nice if you could access that functionality from a web page? With an embedded WebView control, you can.

The key is the addJavascriptInterface() method in the WebView class. You can use it to extend the Document Object Model (DOM) inside the embedded browser and to define a new object that JavaScript code can access. When the JavaScript code invokes methods on that object, it will actually be invoking methods in your Android program.

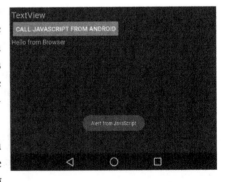

You can call JavaScript methods from your Android program too. All you have to do is call the loadUrl() method, passing it a URL of the form javascript:*code-to-execute*. Instead of going to a new page, the browser will execute the given JavaScript expression inside the current page. You can call a method, change JavaScript variables, modify the browser document—anything you need.

The Dangers of Calling Java from JavaScript

Whenever you allow a web page to access local resources or call functions outside the browser sandbox, you need to consider the security implications very carefully. For example, you wouldn't want to create a method to allow JavaScript to read data from any arbitrary path name because that might expose some private data to a malicious site that knew about your method and your filenames.

Here are a few things to keep in mind. First, don't rely on security by obscurity. Enforce limits on the pages that can use your methods and on the things those methods can do. And remember the golden rule of security: *don't rule things out; rule them in.* In other words, don't try to check for all the bad things that someone can ask you to do (for example, invalid characters in a query). You're bound to miss something. Instead, disallow everything, and pass only the good things you know are safe (that is, test that only valid characters appear).

To demonstrate calls between JavaScript in the WebView and Java in the Android program, let's build a program that is half HTML/JavaScript and half Android (see the previous figure). The top part of the application window is a WebView control, and the bottom part is a TextView and Button from the Android user interface. When you click the buttons and links, it makes calls between the two environments.

Start by creating a "Hello, Android" program using these parameters:

```
Application name: LocalBrowser
Company Domain: example.org
Form factors: Phone and Tablet
Minimum SDK: API 16: Android 4.1 (Jelly Bean)
Add activity: Blank Activity
Activity Name: MainActivity
Layout Name: activity_main
Title: Local Browser
```

The user interface for this program will be split into two parts. The first part is defined in the Android layout file, res/layout/activity_main.xml:

localBrowser/src/main/res/layout/activity_main.xml
```xml
<?xml version="1.0" encoding="utf-8"?>
<LinearLayout
    xmlns:android="http://schemas.android.com/apk/res/android"
    android:orientation="vertical"
    android:layout_width="fill_parent"
    android:layout_height="fill_parent">
    <WebView
        android:id="@+id/web_view"
        android:layout_width="fill_parent"
        android:layout_height="fill_parent"
```

```
        android:layout_weight="1.0" />
    <LinearLayout
        android:orientation="vertical"
        android:layout_width="fill_parent"
        android:layout_height="fill_parent"
        android:layout_weight="1.0"
        android:padding="5sp">
        <TextView
            android:layout_width="fill_parent"
            android:layout_height="wrap_content"
            android:textSize="24sp"
            android:text="@string/textview" />
        <Button
            android:id="@+id/button"
            android:text="@string/call_javascript_from_android"
            android:layout_width="wrap_content"
            android:layout_height="wrap_content"
            android:textSize="18sp" />
        <TextView
            android:id="@+id/text_view"
            android:layout_width="fill_parent"
            android:layout_height="wrap_content"
            android:textSize="18sp" />
    </LinearLayout>
</LinearLayout>
```

The second part is the index.html file that will be loaded into the WebView. This file goes in the assets directory, not the res directory, because it's not a compiled resource. Anything in the assets directory is copied verbatim onto local storage when your program is installed. The directory is intended to be used for local copies of HTML, images, and scripts that the browser can view without being connected to the network.

Creating the assets directory is a little tricky in Android Studio. First you have to switch the Project view to Project mode so you can see the real directories by clicking on the mode label at the top of the window. Navigate to app/src/main, right-click on main, select New > Directory, enter the directory name (assets), and press OK. Then switch back to Android mode. Right-click on assets and create a new file from there.

localBrowser/src/main/assets/index.html

```
Line 1  <html>
   -    <head>
   -    <script language="JavaScript">
   -        function callJS(arg) {
   5            document.getElementById('replaceme').innerHTML = arg;
   -        }
   -    </script>
   -    </head>
```

```
  -    <body>
 10    <h2>WebView</h2>
  -    <p>
  -    <a href="#" onclick="window.alert('Alert from JavaScript')">
  -       Display JavaScript alert</a>
  -    </p>
 15    <p>
  -    <a href="#" onclick="window.android.callAndroid('Hello from Browser')">
  -       Call Android from JavaScript</a>
  -    </p>
  -    <p id="replaceme">
 20    </p>
  -    </body>
  -    </html>
```

Line 4 of index.html defines the callJS() function that our Android program will
be calling later. It takes a string argument and inserts it at the *replaceme* tag,
which is at line 19.

In the previous figure, you can see two HTML links. These are defined in the
code starting at line 12. The first one just calls a standard window.alert() function
to open a window displaying a short message. The second link, at line 16,
calls the callAndroid() method on the window.android object. If you loaded this page
into a normal web browser, window.android would be undefined. But since we're
embedding a browser into an Android application, we can define the object
ourselves so the page can use it.

Next we turn to the Android code in the MainActivity class. Here's the basic
outline, including all the imports we'll need later:

```
localBrowser/src/main/java/org/example/localbrowser/MainActivity.java
Line 1 package org.example.localbrowser;
  -
  -    import android.app.Activity;
  -    import android.os.Bundle;
  5    import android.os.Handler;
  -    import android.util.Log;
  -    import android.view.View;
  -    import android.view.View.OnClickListener;
  -    import android.webkit.JavascriptInterface;
 10    import android.webkit.JsResult;
  -    import android.webkit.WebChromeClient;
  -    import android.webkit.WebView;
  -    import android.widget.Button;
  -    import android.widget.TextView;
 15    import android.widget.Toast;
  -
  -    public class MainActivity extends Activity {
  -        private static final String TAG = "LocalBrowser";
```

```
       private final Handler handler = new Handler();
20     private WebView webView;
       private TextView textView;
       private Button button;

       @Override
25     public void onCreate(Bundle savedInstanceState) {
           super.onCreate(savedInstanceState);
           setContentView(R.layout.activity_main);

           // Find the Android controls on the screen
30         webView = (WebView) findViewById(R.id.web_view);
           textView = (TextView) findViewById(R.id.text_view);
           button = (Button) findViewById(R.id.button);
           // Rest of onCreate follows...
       }
35  }
```

Note the initialization of a Handler object at line 19. JavaScript calls come in on a special thread dedicated to the browser, but Android user interface calls can be made only from the main (GUI) thread. We'll use the Handler class to make the transition.

A thread is an execution context where computer code runs sequentially, one statement after another. Thanks to software and hardware techniques, modern operating systems such as Android can run many threads at the same time. One of them is designated the foreground, or GUI, thread, and all user interface operations run there. The rest are called background threads, which are used to perform long-running operations (such as network I/O) without impacting the user experience.

To call Android Java code from JavaScript, you need to define a plain old Java object with one or more methods, like this:

localBrowser/src/main/java/org/example/localbrowser/MainActivity.java
```
/** Object exposed to JavaScript */
private class AndroidBridge {
  @JavascriptInterface // Required in Android 4.2+
  public void callAndroid(final String arg) { // must be final
    handler.post(new Runnable() {
      public void run() {
        Log.d(TAG, "callAndroid(" + arg + ")");
        textView.setText(arg);
      }
    });
  }
}
```

When JavaScript calls the callAndroid() method, the application creates a new Runnable object and posts it on the running queue of the main thread using Handler.post(). As soon as the main thread gets a chance, it will invoke the run() method, which will call setText() to change the text on the TextView object. Now it's time to tie everything together in the onCreate() method. First we turn on JavaScript (it's off by default) and register our bridge to JavaScript:

localBrowser/src/main/java/org/example/localbrowser/MainActivity.java
```
// Turn on JavaScript in the embedded browser
webView.getSettings().setJavaScriptEnabled(true);

// Expose a Java object to JavaScript in the browser
webView.addJavascriptInterface(new AndroidBridge(),
    "android");
```

Then we create an anonymous WebChromeClient object and register it with the setWebChromeClient() method:

localBrowser/src/main/java/org/example/localbrowser/MainActivity.java
```
// Set up a function to be called when JavaScript tries
// to open an alert window
webView.setWebChromeClient(new WebChromeClient() {
    @Override
    public boolean onJsAlert(final WebView view,
            final String url, final String message,
            JsResult result) {
        Log.d(TAG, "onJsAlert(" + view + ", " + url + ", "
            + message + ", " + result + ")");
        Toast.makeText(MainActivity.this, message, Toast.LENGTH_LONG).show();
        result.confirm();
        return true; // I handled it
    }
});
```

The term *chrome* here refers to all the trimmings around a browser window. If this were a full-blown browser client, we'd need to handle navigation, bookmarks, menus, and so forth. In this case, all we want to do is change what happens with JavaScript code when the browser tries to open a JavaScript alert (using window.alert()). Inside onJsAlert() we use the Android Toast class to create a message window that will appear for a short amount of time.

Once we finish configuring the WebView, we can use loadUrl() to load the local web page:

localBrowser/src/main/java/org/example/localbrowser/MainActivity.java
```
// Load the web page from a local asset
webView.loadUrl("file:///android_asset/index.html");
```

URLs of the form "file:///android_asset/*filename*" (note the three forward slashes) have a special meaning to Android's browser engine. As you might have guessed, they refer to files in the assets directory. In this case, we're loading the index.html file defined earlier.

Here's the res/values/strings.xml file for the LocalBrowser example:

localBrowser/src/main/res/values/strings.xml
```xml
<?xml version="1.0" encoding="utf-8"?>
<resources>
    <string name="app_name">LocalBrowser</string>
    <string name="action_settings">Settings</string>
    <string name="textview">TextView</string>
    <string name="call_javascript_from_android">
        Call JavaScript from Android
    </string>
</resources>
```

The last thing we have to do is wire up the button at the bottom of the screen so it will make a JavaScript call (a call from Java to JavaScript):

localBrowser/src/main/java/org/example/localbrowser/MainActivity.java
```java
// This function will be called when the user presses the
// button on the Android side
button.setOnClickListener(new OnClickListener() {
    public void onClick(View view) {
        Log.d(TAG, "onClick(" + view + ")");
        webView.loadUrl("javascript:callJS('Hello from Android')");
    }
});
```

To do that, we set a listener for button clicks using setOnClickListener(). When the button is pressed, onClick() is called, which turns around and calls Web-View.loadUrl(), passing it a JavaScript expression to evaluate in the browser. The expression is a call to the callJS() function defined in index.html.

Run the program now, and try it. When you click "Display JavaScript alert," an Android message window will appear. When you click "Call Android from JavaScript," the string "Hello from Browser" will be displayed in an Android text control. And finally, when you press the "Call JavaScript from Android" button, the string "Hello from Android" is sent to the browser and inserted in the HTML where it will be displayed at the end of the web page.

Fast-Forward >>

In this chapter, you learned two ways to display web content: by starting a new intent to open a web browser, and by embedding a web viewer in your app. You also learned how to view local content with the viewer, and how to communicate back and forth with between the web page and Java using JavaScript. This technique is used by cross-platform toolkits like Apache Cordova.[7]

Sometimes you don't need to display a web page, but you just need to access some kind of web service or other data from a server. In the next chapter, you'll learn how to do this.

If, on the other hand, you're looking for a program you can take for a walk, you can skip ahead to Chapter 12, *Using Google Play Services*, on page 169.

---

7.   http://cordova.apache.org

Calling Web Services

In recent years, more and more functionality has moved into the cloud. Amazon Web Services is a multibillion-dollar business offering cloud-based computing power and storage. Google Apps handle back-office functionality for millions of small and medium-sized businesses. Microsoft is even in the process of turning its ubiquitous Office suite into a cloud service. One thing all these platforms have in common are REST-ful web service interfaces.

REST (REpresentational State Transfer) means many things to different people, but the most pragmatic definition is a technique of building a service on the Internet that you can cause to do something by making simple HTTP (HyperText Transfer Protocol) requests over TCP/IP (Transmission Control Protocol/Internet Protocol) connections. In the most basic terms, there's a server running out there on the web somewhere, which you can connect to over a standard communications port, using a standard protocol, and you can send it requests and commands and get results back.

Web servers such as google.com and microsoft.com that you use every day are a kind of web service. The client (browser) opens a connection on port 80 or 443, sends it a request for a web page or other asset, receives the result, and then closes the connection. On this simple architecture, the entire World Wide Web is built.

In this chapter you'll learn how to make network connections to services on the web from your Android program. This will open up a new world of functionality to your app.

Using Web Services

Android provides a full set of Java-standard networking APIs, such as the java.net.HttpURLConnection package, that you can use in your programs. The tricky part is to make the calls asynchronously so that your program's user interface is responsive at all times.

Consider what would happen if you just make a blocking network call in the middle of your user interface code. Suddenly your application would not be able to respond to any events such as touches or button presses. It would appear hung to the user. Obviously, that's something you want to avoid.

The java.util.concurrent package is perfect for this kind of work. First created by Doug Lea as a stand-alone library and later incorporated into Java 5, this package supports concurrent programming at a higher level than the regular Java Thread class. The ExecutorService class manages one or more threads for you, and all you have to do is submit tasks (instances of Runnable or Callable) to the executor to have them run. An instance of the Future class is returned, which is a reference to some as-yet-unknown future value that will be returned by your task (if any). You can limit the number of threads that are created, and you can interrupt running tasks if necessary.

To illustrate these concepts, let's create a fun little program that calls the Google Suggest API. Have you ever noticed that when you go to a search site like google.com or bing.com and you start typing in a search term, you immediately start seeing suggestions for how to complete the phrase you're typing? For example, if you type in the letters "and" you might see some suggestions having to do with Android. This is implemented with a web service.

The way it works is that as you type each character into the search box, the browser or web page makes a call to the server to see what could possibly start with the letters you've typed so far. So first you type an "a" and it returns a few likely phrases that begin with a. Then you type an "n" and it gets some phrases that begin with an. And so forth.

Inside the server, it's doing something very clever. Because it knows who you are, where you are, and what you've searched for recently, it customizes the results especially for you. Try this experiment: you and a friend put your computers side by side and go to the same search site. Start typing the same phrase a letter at a time and compare the suggestions. Chances are that they'll be wildly different. The final result from the search after you press Enter will be different too.[1]

---

1. For more information on this phenomenon, see http://en.wikipedia.org/wiki/Filter_bubble.

The Suggest Example

We're going to create a program that calls the Suggest web service and displays the results just like a search engine or smart address bar would. To use this program, simply start typing a phrase. As you type, the program will use the Suggest web service to fetch suggestions about what comes next.

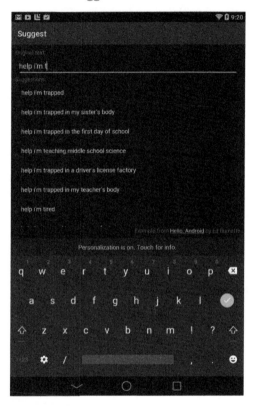

To create this application, start with a "Hello, Android" application using these parameters:

```
Application name: Suggest
Company Domain: example.org
Form factors: Phone and Tablet
Minimum SDK: API 16: Android 4.1 (Jelly Bean)
Add activity: Blank Activity
Activity Name: MainActivity
Layout Name: activity_main
Title: Suggest
```

Since this example accesses the Internet to make a web service call, we need to tell Android to grant us permission.

Add this line to AndroidManifest.xml before the <application> XML tag:

suggest/src/main/AndroidManifest.xml
```
<uses-permission android:name="android.permission.INTERNET" />
```

The layout for the main activity is pretty simple: a vertical LinearLayout that contains several rows:

suggest/src/main/res/layout/activity_main.xml
```
<?xml version="1.0" encoding="utf-8"?>
<LinearLayout xmlns:android="http://schemas.android.com/apk/res/android"
    android:layout_width="fill_parent"
    android:layout_height="fill_parent"
    android:orientation="vertical"
    android:padding="10dip" >

    <TextView
        android:layout_width="fill_parent"
        android:layout_height="wrap_content"
        android:text="@string/original_label" />

    <EditText
        android:id="@+id/original_text"
        android:layout_width="fill_parent"
        android:layout_height="wrap_content"
        android:hint="@string/original_hint"
        android:inputType="textNoSuggestions"
        android:padding="10dip"
        android:textSize="18sp" />

    <TextView
        android:layout_width="fill_parent"
        android:layout_height="wrap_content"
        android:text="@string/result_label" />

    <ListView
        android:id="@+id/result_list"
        android:layout_width="fill_parent"
        android:layout_height="0dp"
        android:layout_weight="1" />

    <TextView
        android:id="@+id/eband_text"
        android:layout_width="fill_parent"
        android:layout_height="wrap_content"
        android:gravity="bottom|right"
        android:text="@string/eband" />

</LinearLayout>
```

In this example, we have five rows. The first row is a label telling the user what to type in the second row, which is a text input field. The third row is another label, followed by the list of suggestions. I wanted to publish this example in the Play Store, so the last row is a little advertisement for the book.

Now let's start modifying the MainActivity class. Here's the basic outline:

suggest/src/main/java/org/example/suggest/MainActivity.java
```
Line 1  package org.example.suggest;

   -    import java.util.ArrayList;
   -    import java.util.List;
   5    import java.util.concurrent.ExecutorService;
   -    import java.util.concurrent.Executors;
   -    import java.util.concurrent.Future;
   -    import java.util.concurrent.RejectedExecutionException;
   -
   10   import android.app.Activity;
   -    import android.app.SearchManager;
   -    import android.content.Intent;
   -    import android.os.Bundle;
   -    import android.os.Handler;
   15   import android.text.Editable;
   -    import android.text.TextWatcher;
   -    import android.text.method.LinkMovementMethod;
   -    import android.view.View;
   -    import android.widget.AdapterView;
   20   import android.widget.AdapterView.OnItemClickListener;
   -    import android.widget.ArrayAdapter;
   -    import android.widget.EditText;
   -    import android.widget.ListView;
   -    import android.widget.TextView;
   25
   -    public class MainActivity extends Activity {
   -        private EditText origText;
   -        private ListView suggList;
   -        private TextView ebandText;
   30
   -        private Handler guiThread;
   -        private ExecutorService suggThread;
   -        private Runnable updateTask;
   -        private Future<?> suggPending;
   35       private List<String> items;
   -        private ArrayAdapter<String> adapter;
   -
   -        @Override
   -        public void onCreate(Bundle savedInstanceState) {
   40           super.onCreate(savedInstanceState);
   -
```

```
  -           setContentView(R.layout.activity_main);
  -           initThreading();
  -           findViews();
 45           setListeners();
  -           setAdapters();
  -
  -      }
  - }
```

After declaring a few variables, we define the onCreate() method starting at line 39 to initialize the threading and user interface. Don't worry; we'll fill out all those other methods it calls as we go.

The findViews() method, called from line 44, just gets a handle to all the user interface elements defined in the layout file:

suggest/src/main/java/org/example/suggest/MainActivity.java
```
private void findViews() {
    origText = (EditText) findViewById(R.id.original_text);
    suggList = (ListView) findViewById(R.id.result_list);
    ebandText = (TextView) findViewById(R.id.eband_text);
}
```

The setAdapters() method, called from onCreate() on line 46, defines a data source for the suggestion list:

suggest/src/main/java/org/example/suggest/MainActivity.java
```
/** Set up adapter for list view. */
private void setAdapters() {
    items = new ArrayList<String>();
    adapter = new ArrayAdapter<String>(this,
            android.R.layout.simple_list_item_1, items);
    suggList.setAdapter(adapter);
}
```

In Android, an Adapter is a class that binds a data source (in this case, the list of suggestions) to a user interface control (in this case, a ListView). We use the standard layouts provided by Android for individual items in the list.

Next we set up the user interface handlers in the setListeners() routine (called from line 45 of onCreate()):

suggest/src/main/java/org/example/suggest/MainActivity.java
```
private void setListeners() {
    // Define listener for text change
    TextWatcher textWatcher = new TextWatcher() {
        public void beforeTextChanged(CharSequence s, int start,
                int count, int after) {
            /* Do nothing */
        }
        public void onTextChanged(CharSequence s, int start,
```

```
            int before, int count) {
         queueUpdate(1000 /* milliseconds */);
      }
      public void afterTextChanged(Editable s) {
         /* Do nothing */
      }
   };

   // Set listener on the original text field
   origText.addTextChangedListener(textWatcher);

   // Define listener for clicking on an item
   OnItemClickListener clickListener = new OnItemClickListener() {
      @Override
      public void onItemClick(AdapterView<?> parent, View view,
            int position, long id) {
         String query = (String) parent.getItemAtPosition(position);
         doSearch(query);
      }
   };

   // Set listener on the suggestion list
   suggList.setOnItemClickListener(clickListener);

   // Make website link clickable
   ebandText.setMovementMethod(LinkMovementMethod.getInstance());
}

private void doSearch(String query) {
   Intent intent = new Intent(Intent.ACTION_WEB_SEARCH);
   intent.putExtra(SearchManager.QUERY, query);
   startActivity(intent);
}
```

We define two listeners: one that is called when the input text is changed and one that is called when one of the suggestions is clicked. queueUpdate() puts a delayed update request on the main thread's to-do list using a Handler. We arbitrarily use a 1,000-millisecond delay for text changes.

At the end of the function we call the setMovementMethod() method on the advertisement view. This makes the hyperlink in the ad text live. If the user taps on the link, a browser window will open on that address.

Threading the Needle

The update request is defined inside the initThreading() method:

suggest/src/main/java/org/example/suggest/MainActivity.java
```
Line 1  private void initThreading() {
   -       guiThread = new Handler();
```

```
-          suggThread = Executors.newSingleThreadExecutor();
-
5          // This task gets suggestions and updates the screen
-          updateTask = new Runnable() {
-             public void run() {
-                // Get text to suggest
-                String original = origText.getText().toString().trim();
10
-                // Cancel previous suggestion if there was one
-                if (suggPending != null)
-                   suggPending.cancel(true);
-
15                // Check to make sure there is text to work on
-                if (original.length() != 0) {
-                   // Let user know we're doing something
-                   setText(R.string.working);
-
20                   // Begin suggestion now but don't wait for it
-                   try {
-                      SuggestTask suggestTask = new SuggestTask(
-                         MainActivity.this, // reference to activity
-                         original // original text
25                      );
-                      suggPending = suggThread.submit(suggestTask);
-                   } catch (RejectedExecutionException e) {
-                      // Unable to start new task
-                      setText(R.string.error);
30                   }
-                }
-             }
-          };
-       }
```

We have two threads: the main Android thread used for the user interface and a suggest thread that we'll create for running the actual suggestion job. We represent the first one with an Android Handler and the second with Java's ExecutorService.

Line 6 defines the update task, which will be scheduled by the queueUpdate() method. When it gets to run, it first fetches the current input text and then prepares to send a suggestion job to the suggest thread. It cancels any suggestion that's already in progress (on line 13), takes care of the case where there's no input text (line 16), and fills in the two text controls where translated text will appear with the string "Working..." (line 18). That text will be replaced later by the actual suggested text.

Finally, on line 22, we create an instance of SuggestTask. We give it a reference to the main activity so it can call back to change the text. We also pass in a

> \|/   **Joe asks:**
> ᠌ᠥ   ## Is All This Delay and Threading Stuff Really Necessary?
>
> One reason you need to do it this way is to avoid making too many calls to the external web service. Imagine what happens as the user enters the word *scissors*. The program sees the word typed in a character at a time, first *s*, then *c*, then *i*, and so on, possibly with backspaces because nobody can remember how to spell *scissors*. Do you want to make a web service request for every character? Not really. Besides putting unnecessary load on the server, it would be wasteful in terms of power. Each request requires the device's radio to transmit and receive several data packets, which uses up a bit of battery power. You want to wait until users finish typing before sending the request, but how do you tell when they're done?
>
> The algorithm used here is that as soon as the user types a letter, a delayed request is started. If the user doesn't type another letter before the one-second delay is up, then the request goes through. Otherwise, the first request is removed from the request queue before it goes out. If the request is already in progress, we try to interrupt it. The good news is that now that I've done it once for you, you can use the same pattern in your own asynchronous programs.

string containing the original text. Line 26 submits the new task to the suggestion thread, returning a reference to the value that will be eventually returned as a Future. In this case, we don't really have a return value since SuggestTask changes the GUI directly, but we use the Future reference back on line 13 to cancel the translation if necessary.

Loose Ends

To finish up the Suggest example, here are a few utility functions used in other places:

suggest/src/main/java/org/example/suggest/MainActivity.java

```java
/** Request an update to start after a short delay */
private void queueUpdate(long delayMillis) {
    // Cancel previous update if it hasn't started yet
    guiThread.removeCallbacks(updateTask);
    // Start an update if nothing happens after a few milliseconds
    guiThread.postDelayed(updateTask, delayMillis);
}

/** Modify list on the screen (called from another thread) */
public void setSuggestions(List<String> suggestions) {
    guiSetList(suggList, suggestions);
}
```

```
/** All changes to the GUI must be done in the GUI thread */
private void guiSetList(final ListView view,
        final List<String> list) {
    guiThread.post(new Runnable() {
        public void run() {
            setList(list);
        }

    });
}

/** Display a message */
private void setText(int id) {
    adapter.clear();
    adapter.add(getResources().getString(id));
}

/** Display a list */
private void setList(List<String> list) {
    adapter.clear();
    adapter.addAll(list);
}
```

queueUpdate() puts an update request on the main thread's request queue but tells it to wait a little while before actually running it. If there was already a request on the queue, it's removed.

The setSuggestions() method is being used by SuggestTask to update the user interface when results come back from the web service. It calls a private function named guiSetList(), which uses the Handler.post() method to ask the main GUI thread to update the list control. This extra step is necessary because you can't call user interface functions from non-user-interface threads, and guiSetList() will be called by the translate thread.

Finally, setText() and setList() update the adapter to contain a single string or a list of strings, respectively.

Here's the res/values/strings.xml file for the Suggest example. It defines the string resources used in the rest of the program:

`suggest/src/main/res/values/strings.xml`
```xml
<?xml version="1.0" encoding="utf-8"?>
<resources>

    <string name="app_name">Suggest</string>
    <string name="action_settings">Settings</string>
    <string name="original_hint">Enter partial text</string>
    <string name="original_label">Original text:</string>
    <string name="result_label">Suggestions:</string>
```

```xml
<string name="working">Working...</string>
<string name="error">(Web service error)</string>
<string name="interrupted">(Web service interrupted)</string>
<string name="no_results">(No suggestions)</string>
<string name="eband">Example from
    <a href="http://pragprog.com/book/eband4">Hello, Android</a>
    by Ed Burnette</string>

</resources>
```

The only missing piece now is the SuggestTask class that performs the web service call in the background.

The Suggest Task

For completeness, here's the definition of SuggestTask:

suggest/src/main/java/org/example/suggest/SuggestTask.java
```java
package org.example.suggest;

import java.io.IOException;
import java.net.HttpURLConnection;
import java.net.URL;
import java.net.URLEncoder;
import java.util.LinkedList;
import java.util.List;

import org.xmlpull.v1.XmlPullParser;
import org.xmlpull.v1.XmlPullParserException;

import android.util.Log;
import android.util.Xml;

public class SuggestTask implements Runnable {
    private static final String TAG = "SuggestTask";
    private final MainActivity suggest;
    private final String original;

    SuggestTask(MainActivity context, String original) {
        this.suggest = context;
        this.original = original;
    }

    public void run() {
        // Get suggestions for the original text
        List<String> suggestions = doSuggest(original);
        suggest.setSuggestions(suggestions);
    }

    /**
     * Call the Google Suggest API to create a list of suggestions
```

```java
 * from a partial string.
 *
 * Note: This isn't really a supported API so if it breaks, try
 * the Yahoo one instead:
 *
 * http://ff.search.yahoo.com/gossip?output=xml&command=WORD or
 * http://ff.search.yahoo.com/gossip?output=fxjson&command=WORD
 */
private List<String> doSuggest(String original) {
    List<String> messages = new LinkedList<String>();
    String error = null;
    HttpURLConnection con = null;
    Log.d(TAG, "doSuggest(" + original + ")");

    try {
        // Check if task has been interrupted
        if (Thread.interrupted())
            throw new InterruptedException();

        // Build RESTful query for Google API
        String q = URLEncoder.encode(original, "UTF-8");
        URL url = new URL(
                "http://google.com/complete/search?output=toolbar&q="
                    + q);
        con = (HttpURLConnection) url.openConnection();
        con.setReadTimeout(10000 /* milliseconds */);
        con.setConnectTimeout(15000 /* milliseconds */);
        con.setRequestMethod("GET");
        con.addRequestProperty("Referer",
            "http://www.pragprog.com/book/eband4");
        con.setDoInput(true);

        // Start the query
        con.connect();

        // Check if task has been interrupted
        if (Thread.interrupted())
            throw new InterruptedException();

        // Read results from the query
        XmlPullParser parser = Xml.newPullParser();
        parser.setInput(con.getInputStream(), null);
        int eventType = parser.getEventType();
        while (eventType != XmlPullParser.END_DOCUMENT) {
            String name = parser.getName();
            if (eventType == XmlPullParser.START_TAG
                    && name.equalsIgnoreCase("suggestion")) {
                for (int i = 0; i < parser.getAttributeCount(); i++) {
                    if (parser.getAttributeName(i).equalsIgnoreCase(
                        "data")) {
```

```
                    messages.add(parser.getAttributeValue(i));
                }
            }
        }
        eventType = parser.next();
    }

    // Check if task has been interrupted
    if (Thread.interrupted())
        throw new InterruptedException();

} catch (IOException e) {
    Log.e(TAG, "IOException", e);
    error = suggest.getResources().getString(R.string.error)
        + " " + e.toString();
} catch (XmlPullParserException e) {
    Log.e(TAG, "XmlPullParserException", e);
    error = suggest.getResources().getString(R.string.error)
        + " " + e.toString();
} catch (InterruptedException e) {
    Log.d(TAG, "InterruptedException", e);
    error = suggest.getResources().getString(
        R.string.interrupted);
} finally {
    if (con != null) {
        con.disconnect();
    }
}

// If there was an error, return the error by itself
if (error != null) {
    messages.clear();
    messages.add(error);
}

// Print something if we got nothing
if (messages.size() == 0) {
    messages.add(suggest.getResources().getString(
        R.string.no_results));
}

// All done
Log.d(TAG, "   -> returned " + messages);
return messages;
    }
}
```

This is a nice example of calling a REST-ful web service using HttpURLConnection, parsing results in JavaScript Object Notation (JSON) format, and handling all sorts of network errors and requests for interruptions. I'm not going to explain it in detail here because it contains nothing Android-specific except for a few debugging messages.

That wraps up the Suggest example. Give it a try to see what kind of interesting things Google thinks you're searching for. You can find more funny search suggestions on the web with a quick search.

Fast-Forward >>

In this chapter, we covered how to use an asynchronous web service. If you're going to do much concurrent programming with classes such as ExecutorService, I recommend *Java Concurrency in Practice [Goe06]* by Brian Goetz.

Creating web services is beyond the scope of this book, but one of the easiest ways is to use the Google App Engine.[2] GAE allows you to host your own back-end services in the cloud using a variety of languages such as Java, Python, and PHP.

The next couple of chapters will explore a new level of interactivity through touch events and Google Services. If you're anxious to learn more about data sources and data binding, you can skip ahead to Chapter 13, *Putting SQL to Work*, on page 183. It covers a different way of taking work off the GUI thread using the Loader class.

---

2. http://developers.google.com/appengine/

CHAPTER 12

Using Google Play Services

Google Play Services is an add-on to the Android framework that can be found on any Android device that uses the Google Play Store.

From its humble beginnings as a way to get access to Google's authorization and Google+ social network, Google Play Services has grown to include a huge array of features, including many that were originally part of the base Android framework. These include:

- Location services
- Game services
- In-app purchases
- Ads
- Mobile analytics
- Maps
- Push messages
- Cloud save
- ...and more.

All Google Play Services are similar in the way you include them in your apps, configure, and call them. Therefore, learning about one service will get you halfway there to using all of them.

This chapter will introduce Google Play Services through the Location Services API. By the end of the chapter you'll know how to include Google Play Services in your app, how to detect when it's not available, how to call it, and how to handle any errors that occur.

How It Works

In your app, you include a small client library that communicates to the Google Play Services APK (application package). When you make a call, it actually sends a message to the service, which does the operation on your behalf.

Every app talks to the same Services APK, which is updated frequently from the Google Play Store. This design allows Google to push fixes and new functionality directly to your phone or tablet without having to wait for Android system updates and carrier approvals. It also saves space because each app doesn't have to contain a repeat of the same code.

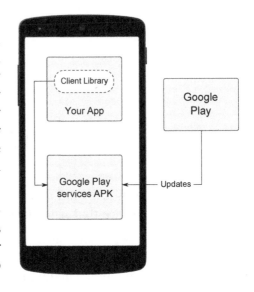

One of the most frequently used features provided by Google Play Services is Location Services. Let's take a closer look to see what it does and how to use it.

Using Location Services

Sensors such as the GPS and accelerometer chips found in nearly every mobile phone have opened a new world of location- and environment-aware mobile computing. These technologies, in combination with trends such as the adoption of broadband mobile Internet and the exponential growth of computing power and storage, are revolutionizing the way we interact with computers and with each other.

The Android framework provides a number of APIs to integrate sensor data into our apps. These include low-level APIs to get location information from GPS, cell towers, and Wi-Fi. Interpreting all that data is not an easy task, but the Location Services API can help. Location Services provides a powerful, high-level framework that all apps can use to get reliable location data, while at the same time reducing the amount of battery power used.

Location Services started out as a custom library used internally by Google Maps and other proprietary applications. By making it a part of Google Play Services, Google lets you use the same technology in your own apps. Now, Google recommends that all new code be written using Location Services.

To show off Location Services, we're going to create an app that displays your current location over time. The following figure shows a screen shot of the finished project.

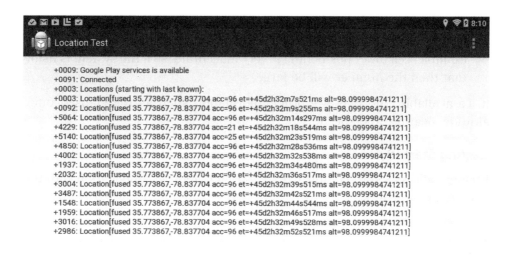

Your initial location is printed, and then every so often the screen is updated with your latest location. Just sitting still, you won't see much of a difference, so this is app is intended to be picked up and taken out for a walk.

So what do all those numbers mean? The first number is the time that elapsed between lines, in milliseconds. This followed by the location, printed as a string. The format of the string is set by the Location.toString() method.

In Java programming, it's common practice to create a toString() method for each of your major classes so that you can easily print them out during debugging. An instance of the Location class prints itself in this form:

```
Location[<provider-type> <longitude>, <latitude>, acc=<accuracy>]
```

where:

provider-type

is the hardware or software provider that computed the location. The "Fused" provider is smart software that combines locations from all the different hardware providers (Wi-Fi, cell tower, etc.) to get the best location for the least amount of power.

longitude, latitude

is the actual current location on a globe.

accuracy

is a measure of how close the system has zeroed-in on your location. For example, cell tower positioning is very inaccurate, so if the system is using that then the number will be large.

If it's available, you may see other information such as the elapsed time, altitude, bearing, and speed.

Getting Started

Enough talk, let's start coding! Create a "Hello, Android" application with the following parameters:

```
Application name: Location Test
Company Domain: example.org
Form factors: Phone and Tablet
Minimum SDK: API 16: Android 4.1 (Jelly Bean)
Add activity: Blank Activity
Activity Name: MainActivity
Layout Name: activity_main
Title: LocationTest
```

Setting up any project to use Google Play Services requires two or three extra steps compared to your run-of-the-mill Android app. First, you need to modify the build script to add a compile-time dependency for the Google Play Services client library. Open the build.gradle file for the "app" module (not the one that says "Project: LocationTest"). Add a new build rule under dependencies for the latest version of play-services. When you're done it should look like this:

locationTest/build.gradle
```
// ...
dependencies {
    compile fileTree(dir: 'libs', include: ['*.jar'])
    compile 'com.android.support:appcompat-v7:22+'
    compile 'com.google.android.gms:play-services:7.+'
}
```

At the top of the window you'll see a warning that says "Gradle files have changed since last project sync." Press the Sync Now link to recompile the project.

The second step involves adding a small piece of information to your manifest file. Open AndroidManifest.xml and add the following tag as a child of the application tag:

locationTest/src/main/AndroidManifest.xml
```
<meta-data
        android:name="com.google.android.gms.version"
        android:value="@integer/google_play_services_version" />
```

There's one more step if you use ProGuard, an application optimization and obfuscation tool. None of the examples in this book use it, but if you do, you will also have to edit the proguard-project.txt file to keep ProGuard from stripping away required classes. See the online doc for full details.[1]

Now that we have the project set up, let's work on the user interface.

Creating the User Interface

The main activity consists of a scrolling Text view that covers the whole screen. Log lines are added to the end, and the text scrolls up when the screen is filled. Edit the layout file, activity_main.xml, so it has a ScrollView with the id scroller containing a TextView with the id output:

```
locationTest/src/main/res/layout/activity_main.xml
<?xml version="1.0" encoding="utf-8"?>
<ScrollView
    xmlns:android="http://schemas.android.com/apk/res/android"
    xmlns:tools="http://schemas.android.com/tools"
    android:id="@+id/scroller"
    android:layout_width="match_parent"
    android:layout_height="match_parent"
    android:paddingLeft="@dimen/activity_horizontal_margin"
    android:paddingRight="@dimen/activity_horizontal_margin"
    android:paddingTop="@dimen/activity_vertical_margin"
    android:paddingBottom="@dimen/activity_vertical_margin"
    tools:context=".MainActivity">

    <TextView
        android:id="@+id/output"
        android:layout_width="match_parent"
        android:layout_height="match_parent"
        android:textSize="16sp" />
</ScrollView>
```

Set the text size to 16sp to make the text a little easier to read.

Next, open MainActivity and create the outline shown here:

```
locationTest/src/main/java/org/example/locationtest/MainActivity.java
Line 1  package org.example.locationtest;
     -
     -  import android.app.Activity;
     -  import android.app.Dialog;
     5  import android.content.Intent;
     -  import android.content.IntentSender;
     -  import android.location.Location;
     -  import android.os.Bundle;
```

---

1. http://d.android.com/google/play-services/setup.html

```
  -   import android.view.Menu;
 10   import android.view.MenuItem;
  -   import android.view.View;
  -   import android.widget.ScrollView;
  -   import android.widget.TextView;
  -
 15   import com.google.android.gms.common.ConnectionResult;
  -   import com.google.android.gms.common.GooglePlayServicesUtil;
  -   import com.google.android.gms.common.api.GoogleApiClient;
  -   import com.google.android.gms.location.LocationListener;
  -   import com.google.android.gms.location.LocationRequest;
 20   import com.google.android.gms.location.LocationServices;
  -
  -   public class MainActivity extends Activity implements
  -       GoogleApiClient.ConnectionCallbacks,
  -       GoogleApiClient.OnConnectionFailedListener,
 25       LocationListener {
  -       private static final long UPDATE_INTERVAL = 5000;
  -       private static final long FASTEST_INTERVAL = 1000;
  -       private static final int CONNECTION_FAILURE_RESOLUTION_REQUEST = 9000;
  -
 30       private TextView mOutput;
  -       private ScrollView mScroller;
  -       private GoogleApiClient mGoogleApiClient;
  -       private long mLastTime;
  -       // ...
 35   }
```

All the imports that this class needs start on line 3. If you're typing in this example as you go, you can leave them out and have Android Studio automatically add them later when you press Alt+Enter on each undefined reference.

The MainActivity class starts on line 22. It's a subclass of the Activity class, and in addition, it implements two interfaces: ConnectionCallbacks and OnConnectionFailedListener. Implementing the interfaces tells the compiler that we'll be adding some required methods that are part of those interfaces. Until we put those in, you may see error markers in your editor window.

Inside MainActivity we declare some constants and variables that will be needed later on.

Now that we have the basic outline, let's start filling in the missing methods. The first one is the onCreate() method that's called before the activity is started:

locationTest/src/main/java/org/example/locationtest/MainActivity.java

```
Line 1   @Override
  -   public void onCreate(Bundle savedInstanceState) {
  -       super.onCreate(savedInstanceState);
  -       setContentView(R.layout.activity_main);
  5
```

```
   -        // Define new API client
   -        mGoogleApiClient = new GoogleApiClient.Builder(this)
   -                .addConnectionCallbacks(this)
   -                .addOnConnectionFailedListener(this)
  10                .addApi(LocationServices.API)
   -                .build();
   -
   -        // Get view references
   -        mOutput = (TextView) findViewById(R.id.output);
  15        mScroller = (ScrollView) findViewById(R.id.scroller);
   -
   -        // Get current time so we can tell how far apart the updates are
   -        mLastTime = System.currentTimeMillis();
   -    }
```

The first thing it does on line 4 is to fill the activity with the inflated layout XML. On line 7 it defines a new GoogleApiClient, a class in Google Play Services that we'll connect to later to get locations.

On line 14 we call findViewById() to get a handle to the two views in the layout. Finally on line 18 we get the current system time so we can tell how much time has elapsed between each line printed to the log.

The Blank Activity template added these two methods for you:

locationTest/src/main/java/org/example/locationtest/MainActivity.java

```
Line 1  @Override
   -    public boolean onCreateOptionsMenu(Menu menu) {
   -        // Inflate the menu; this adds items to the action bar if it is present.
   -        getMenuInflater().inflate(R.menu.menu_main, menu);
   5        return true;
   -    }
   -
   -    @Override
   -    public boolean onOptionsItemSelected(MenuItem item) {
  10        // Handle action bar item clicks here. The action bar will
   -        // automatically handle clicks on the Home/Up button, so long
   -        // as you specify a parent activity in AndroidManifest.xml.
   -        int id = item.getItemId();
   -        if (id == R.id.action_settings) {
  15            return true;
   -        }
   -        return super.onOptionsItemSelected(item);
   -    }
```

They implement a Settings menu that could be used to add options to the program. For example, you could add an option to control how often the location should be updated or how accurate it should be. I'll leave that as an exercise for the reader. For now you can just leave them as they are.

Location, Location, Location

We want to set it up so that we connect to the location provider when the user opens the app or switches to it from another app. And then, when the user switches out of the app we want to disconnect. The best place to do that is in the onResume() and onPause() methods:

```
locationTest/src/main/java/org/example/locationtest/MainActivity.java
@Override
protected void onResume() {
    super.onResume();
    // Connect the client if Google Services are available
    if (servicesAvailable()) {
        mGoogleApiClient.connect();
    }
}

@Override
protected void onPause() {
    if (mGoogleApiClient.isConnected()) {
        mGoogleApiClient.disconnect();
    }
    super.onPause();
}
```

Inside onResume() we check to see if Google Play Services is available. If it is, then we call the connect() method on the Google API client that we created in onCreate(). To bookend the connection, in onPause() we check to see if we're connected, and if so, we disconnect.

Calling the connect method has an important side effect. Once the connection is complete, Location Services will call the onConnected() method in your class. Here's how you can define it:

```
locationTest/src/main/java/org/example/locationtest/MainActivity.java
Line 1  /**
   -     * Called by Location Services when the request to connect the
   -     * client finishes successfully. At this point, you can
   -     * request the current location or start periodic updates.
   5     */
   -    @Override
   -    public void onConnected(Bundle dataBundle) {
   -        // Display the connection status
   -        log("Connected");
   10
   -        // Get current location
   -        Location location = LocationServices.FusedLocationApi.getLastLocation(
   -                mGoogleApiClient);
   -        log("Locations (starting with last known):");
```

```
15    if (location != null) {
  -       dumpLocation(location);
  -    }
  -    // ...
- }
```

The log() method adds one line to the output view and scrolls it up. The dumpLocation() method converts a location to a string and logs it:

locationTest/src/main/java/org/example/locationtest/MainActivity.java
```
/** Write a string to the output window */
private void log(String string) {
   long newTime = System.currentTimeMillis();
   mOutput.append(String.format("+%04d: %s\n",
         newTime - mLastTime, string));
   mLastTime = newTime;

   // A little trick to make the text view scroll to the end
   mScroller.post(new Runnable() {
      @Override
      public void run() {
         mScroller.fullScroll(View.FOCUS_DOWN);
      }
   });
}

/** Describe the given location, which might be null */
private void dumpLocation(Location location) {
   if (location == null)
      log("Location[unknown]");
   else
      log(location.toString());
}
```

Note that we get the current time before printing each log message, subtract it from the last time, and print the difference at the beginning of the line.

Getting Updates

As currently written, the program only displays your location once when it starts up. We want it to keep printing the location every so often so that the log will get longer and show all the places you've been while you move around. You can do that with three easy changes.

First, at the end of onConnected() method, you call a method using the API client to request that we get updates.

Here's the code:

locationTest/src/main/java/org/example/locationtest/MainActivity.java
```java
public void onConnected(Bundle dataBundle) {
    // ...
    // Request update every 1-5 seconds, high accuracy
    LocationRequest locationRequest = LocationRequest.create();
    locationRequest.setPriority(LocationRequest.PRIORITY_HIGH_ACCURACY);
    locationRequest.setInterval(UPDATE_INTERVAL);
    locationRequest.setFastestInterval(FASTEST_INTERVAL);
    LocationServices.FusedLocationApi.requestLocationUpdates(
            mGoogleApiClient, locationRequest, this);
}
```

In this example, we request a priority that favors accuracy over power consumption, and an update interval of at least 5 seconds. If another app that's also using Location Services happens to get a location before 5 seconds are up, then we'll get them more often. However, we set a "fastest interval" to tell the system that we don't want to get more than one update per second.

Note that these settings are hints. The system will do its best to respect your wishes, but in order to save power it may take a few liberties. That means you should be prepared for updates that occur a little more or less frequently than you requested. You can clearly see this when you run the app and look at the times printed on each line.

When an update is available, the onLocationChanged() method will be called:

locationTest/src/main/java/org/example/locationtest/MainActivity.java
```java
@Override
public void onLocationChanged(Location location) {
    dumpLocation(location);
}
```

All it does is print the location to the log view.

Handling Errors

Devices without the Play Store, notably Amazon Kindle Fire devices, don't have Google Play Services. In the onResume() method we called servicesAvailable() to see if the services are installed and up to date. Here's the definition of that method:

locationTest/src/main/java/org/example/locationtest/MainActivity.java
```java
/** Check that Google Play Services is available */
private boolean servicesAvailable() {
    int resultCode = GooglePlayServicesUtil.
            isGooglePlayServicesAvailable(this);
    if (ConnectionResult.SUCCESS == resultCode) {
        log("Google Play services is available");
        return true;
```

```
   } else {
      log("Google Play services is not available");
      showErrorDialog(resultCode);
      return false;
   }
}
```

If the services aren't available, then we call the showErrorDialog() method:

locationTest/src/main/java/org/example/locationtest/MainActivity.java
```
/** Show a Google Play Services error message */
private void showErrorDialog(int resultCode) {
   // Get the error dialog from Google Play Services
   Dialog errorDialog = GooglePlayServicesUtil.getErrorDialog(
         resultCode, this, CONNECTION_FAILURE_RESOLUTION_REQUEST);

   if (errorDialog != null) {
      // Display error
      errorDialog.show();
   }
}
```

The Services client library provides a function to create an error dialog to show to the user.

An error can also occur when trying to connect to the Location service. Because the connection can take some time to complete, remember that if the connection succeeded it called the onConnected() method in our activity. If it failed, then the onConnectionFailed() method will be called instead.

locationTest/src/main/java/org/example/locationtest/MainActivity.java
```
/**
 * Called by Location Services if the attempt to connect to the
 * location client fails.
 */
@Override
public void onConnectionFailed(ConnectionResult connectionResult) {
   // Can it be resolved, for example by installing a new version?
   log("Connection failed");
   if (connectionResult.hasResolution()) {
      try {
         // Start an Activity that tries to resolve the error
         log("Trying to resolve the error...");
         connectionResult.startResolutionForResult(
               this, CONNECTION_FAILURE_RESOLUTION_REQUEST);
      } catch (IntentSender.SendIntentException e) {
         log("Exception during resolution: " + e.toString());
      }
   } else {
      // No resolution is available
      showErrorDialog(connectionResult.getErrorCode());
```

```
    }
}

/**
 * Called by Location Services when the client is temporarily in a
 * disconnected state.
 */
@Override
public void onConnectionSuspended(int cause) {
    log("Connection suspended");
}
```

Suppose Google Play Services is available but it's not the expected version (set in the metadata in AndroidManifest.xml). In this case, we can attempt to resolve the error and try again. A dialog will appear offering the user the option of going to the Play Store and getting the right version. After the user does that, the onActivityResult() method will be called:

locationTest/src/main/java/org/example/locationtest/MainActivity.java
```
/** Handle resolution results from Google Play Services */
@Override
protected void onActivityResult(int requestCode, int resultCode,
                                Intent data) {
    // Decide what to do based on the original request code
    switch (requestCode) {
        case CONNECTION_FAILURE_RESOLUTION_REQUEST:
            // If the result code is OK, try to connect again
            log("Resolution result code is: " + resultCode);
            switch (resultCode) {
                case Activity.RESULT_OK:
                    // Try to connect again here
                    mGoogleApiClient.connect();
                    break;
            }
            break;
    }
}
```

This method is called whenever one activity starts another and expects to get some kind of result back. So first we have to check to see if the request code matches the one we set in onConnectionFailed(). Then we have to check that the resolution worked (resultcode is OK). If all that matches, then we can try to do the connect call again. It should work the second time.

Asking for Permission

The final step is to add these lines to AndroidManifest.xml before the application tag:

`locationTest/src/main/AndroidManifest.xml`

```
<uses-permission
    android:name="android.permission.ACCESS_COARSE_LOCATION" />
<uses-permission
    android:name="android.permission.ACCESS_FINE_LOCATION" />
```

This tells Android that the app needs to access the user's current position in order to run.

Time for Walkies

Now that all the methods are defined, you should have no errors in the editor window. Run the program, and you should see the updates scrolling by, just like the sample screenshot on page 171. Note that the program requires a working location provider to work so you'll need to run it on a real device.

Notice how the interval between log entries varies quite a lot. Location Services will try to keep them between 1000 and 5000 milliseconds (1–5 seconds) but it doesn't always succeed.

Assuming you're running the app on a real device, unplug it and take it outdoors for a stroll. You should see the latitude, longitude, and accuracy change as you move around.

Looking at these numbers may be boring, but now that you have them, there's no limit to what you can do. Why not use the Maps API to draw a trail of where you've been today? Or use the Geolocation API to show your progress in terms of street addresses? You could even set off an alarm when you get close to your favorite coffee shop. All these things are possible with Google APIs and a little keyboard grease.

Bonus exercise: Let this app run for a long time. It will get slower and slower until it's almost unresponsive. Figure out why, and how to fix it.

Fast-Forward >>

This chapter introduced you to the exciting capabilities of Google Play Services. We created an app using one of those services (Location), but that's just scratching the surface. To learn more, consult the online documentation.[2]

We're getting close to the end of this book—just one more chapter to go. The next chapter will show you how to use SQL to store structured information (for example, a travel log of locations, photographs, and notes) locally on your mobile phone.

---

2. http://d.android.com/google/play-services

CHAPTER 13

Putting SQL to Work

For the past thirty years, databases have been a staple of enterprise application development, but until recently they were too expensive and unwieldy for smaller-scale use. That has changed with small embedded engines such as the one included with the Android platform.

This chapter will show you how to use Android's embedded database engine, SQLite. You'll also learn how to use Android's data binding to connect your data sources to your user interface. You'll look at the ContentProvider class, which allows two applications to share the same data.

You can use ContentProviders and SQLite in your own apps to hold lists of addresses, orders, moves in a game, or a variety of other objects. Any time you have to remember more than a few items across program invocations, these techniques will come in handy.

As a bonus, I'll show you how to use the Loader class to keep your UI responsive and smooth. Without loaders, database accesses and other long-running tasks can cause pauses in your user interface, leading to a bad experience for the user.

Introducing SQLite

SQLite[1] is a tiny yet powerful database engine created by Dr. Richard Hipp in 2000. It is arguably the most widely deployed SQL database engine in the world. Besides Android, SQLite can be found in the Apple iPhone, Symbian phones, Mozilla Firefox, Skype, PHP, Adobe AIR, Mac OS X, Solaris, and many other places.

---

1.   http://www.sqlite.org

> ## SQLite License
>
> The SQLite source code contains no license because it's in the public domain. Instead of a license, the source offers you this blessing:
>
> *May you do good and not evil.*
>
> *May you find forgiveness for yourself and forgive others.*
>
> *May you share freely, never taking more than you give.*

There are three reasons why it's so popular:

- It's free. The authors have placed it in the public domain and don't charge for its use.

- It's small. The current version is about 150 KB, well within the memory budget of an Android phone.

- It requires no setup or administration. There's no server, no config file, and no need for a database administrator.

A SQLite database is just a file. You can take that file, move it around, and even copy it to another system (for example, from your phone to your workstation), and it will work fine. Android stores the database file in the /data/data/*packagename*/databases directory. You can use the adb command to view, move, or delete it.

Instead of calling Java I/O routines to access this file from your program, you run Structured Query Language (SQL) statements. Through its helper classes and convenience methods, Android hides some of the syntax from you, but you still need to know a bit of SQL to use it.

SQL 101

If you've used Oracle, SQL Server, MySQL, DB2, or other database engines, then SQL should be old hat to you. You can skip this section and go to *Hello, Database*, on page 186. For the rest of you, here's a quick refresher.

To use a SQL database, you submit SQL statements and get back results. There are three main types of SQL statements: DDL, Modification, and Query.

DDL Statements

A database file can have any number of tables. A table consists of rows, and each row has a certain number of columns. Each column of the table has a name and a data type (text string, number, and so forth). You define these tables and column names by first running Data Definition Language (DDL) statements. Here's a statement that creates a table with three columns:

sqlite/create.sql
```
create table mytable (
  _id integer primary key autoincrement,
  name text,
  phone text );
```

One of the columns is designated as the PRIMARY KEY, a number that uniquely identifies the row. AUTOINCREMENT means that the database will add 1 to the key for every record to make sure it's unique. By convention, the first column is always called _id. The _id column isn't strictly required for SQLite, but later when we want to use an Android ContentProvider, we'll need it.

Note that, unlike most databases, in SQLite the column types are just hints. If you try to store a string in an integer column, or vice versa, it will just work with no complaints. The SQLite authors consider this to be a feature, not a bug.

Modification Statements

SQL provides a number of statements that let you insert, delete, and update records in the database. For example, to add a few phone numbers, you could use this:

sqlite/insert.sql
```
insert into mytable values(null, 'Steven King', '555-1212');
insert into mytable values(null, 'John Smith', '555-2345');
insert into mytable values(null, 'Fred Smitheizen', '555-4321');
```

The values are specified in the same order you used in the CREATE TABLE statement. We specify NULL for _id because SQLite figures that value out for us.

Query Statements

Once data has been loaded into a table, you run queries against the table using a SELECT statement. For example, if you wanted to get the third entry, you could do this:

sqlite/selectid.sql
```
select * from mytable where(_id=3);
```

It's more likely you'd want to look up a person's phone number by name. Here's how you'd find all the records containing "Smith" in the name:

sqlite/selectwhere.sql
```
select name, phone from mytable where(name like "%smith%");
```

Keep in mind that SQL is case insensitive. Keywords, column names, and even search strings can be specified in either uppercase or lowercase.

Now you know just enough about SQL to be dangerous. Let's see how to put that knowledge to work in a simple program.

Hello, Database

To demonstrate SQLite, let's create a little application called Events that stores records in a database and displays them later. We're going to start simple and build up from there. Open a new "Hello, Android" program using these values in the project wizard:

```
Application name: Events
Company Domain: example.org
Form factors: Phone and Tablet
Minimum SDK: API 16: Android 4.1 (Jelly Bean)
Add activity: Blank Activity
Activity Name: MainActivity
Layout Name: activity_main
Title: Events
```

As always, you can download the complete source code from the book's website[2] (look for the eventsv1 example).

We need somewhere to hold a few constants describing the database, so let's create a Constants interface:

```
eventsv1/src/main/java/org/example/events/Constants.java
package org.example.events;
import android.provider.BaseColumns;
public interface Constants extends BaseColumns {
    public static final String TABLE_NAME = "events";
    // Columns in the Events database
    public static final String TIME = "time";
    public static final String TITLE = "title";
}
```

Each event will be stored as a row in the events table. Each row will have _id, time, and title columns. _id is the primary key, declared in the BaseColumns interface that we extend. time and title will be used for a time stamp and event title, respectively.

---

2. http://pragprog.com/book/eband4

Using SQLiteOpenHelper

Next we'll create a helper class called EventsData to represent the database itself. This class extends the Android SQLiteOpenHelper class, which manages database creation and versions. All you need to do is provide a constructor and override two methods.

eventsv1/src/main/java/org/example/events/EventsData.java

```
Line 1   package org.example.events;

         import static android.provider.BaseColumns._ID;
         import static org.example.events.Constants.TABLE_NAME;
      5  import static org.example.events.Constants.TIME;
         import static org.example.events.Constants.TITLE;
         import android.content.Context;
         import android.database.sqlite.SQLiteDatabase;
         import android.database.sqlite.SQLiteOpenHelper;
     10
         public class EventsData extends SQLiteOpenHelper {
             private static final String DATABASE_NAME = "events.db";
             private static final int DATABASE_VERSION = 1;

     15      /** Create a helper object for the Events database */
             public EventsData(Context ctx) {
                 super(ctx, DATABASE_NAME, null, DATABASE_VERSION);
             }

     20      @Override
             public void onCreate(SQLiteDatabase db) {
                 db.execSQL("CREATE TABLE " + TABLE_NAME + " (" + _ID
                         + " INTEGER PRIMARY KEY AUTOINCREMENT, " + TIME
                         + " INTEGER," + TITLE + " TEXT NOT NULL);");
     25      }

             @Override
             public void onUpgrade(SQLiteDatabase db, int oldVersion,
                     int newVersion) {
     30          db.execSQL("DROP TABLE IF EXISTS " + TABLE_NAME);
                 onCreate(db);
             }
         }
```

The constructor starts on line 16. DATABASE_NAME is the actual filename of the database we're using (events.db), and DATABASE_VERSION is just a number we make up. If this were a real program, you would increase the version number whenever you had to make significant changes to the database design (for example, to add a new column).

> **Joe asks:**
> ## Why Is Constants an Interface?
>
> It's a Java thing. I don't know about you, but I dislike having to repeat the class name every time I use a constant. For example, I want to just type TIME and not Constants.TIME. Traditionally, the way to do that in Java is to use interfaces. Classes can inherit from the Constants interface and then leave out the interface name when referencing any fields. If you look at the BaseColumns interface, you'll see the Android programmers used the same trick.
>
> Starting with Java 5, however, there's a better way: static imports. That's the method I'll use in EventsData and other classes in this chapter. Since Constants is an interface, you can use it the old way or the new way as you prefer.

The first time you try to access a database, SQLiteOpenHelper will notice it doesn't exist and call the onCreate() method to create it. On line 21, we override that and run a CREATE TABLE SQL statement. This will create the events table and the events.db database file that contains it.

When Android detects you're referencing an old database (based on the version number), it will call the onUpgrade() method (line 28). In this example, we just delete the old table, but you could do something smarter here if you like. For example, you could run an ALTER TABLE SQL command to add a column to an existing database.

Defining the Main Program

Our first attempt at the Events program will use a local SQLite database to store the events, and it will show them as a string inside a TextView.

Define the layout file (layout/activity_main.xml) as follows:

eventsv1/src/main/res/layout/activity_main.xml
```xml
<?xml version="1.0" encoding="utf-8"?>
<ScrollView
    xmlns:android="http://schemas.android.com/apk/res/android"
    xmlns:tools="http://schemas.android.com/tools"
    android:layout_width="match_parent"
    android:layout_height="match_parent"
    android:paddingLeft="@dimen/activity_horizontal_margin"
    android:paddingRight="@dimen/activity_horizontal_margin"
    android:paddingTop="@dimen/activity_vertical_margin"
    android:paddingBottom="@dimen/activity_vertical_margin"
    tools:context=".MainActivity">
    <TextView
        android:id="@+id/text"
        android:layout_width="match_parent"
```

```
        android:layout_height="wrap_content" />
    </ScrollView>
```

This declares the TextView with an imaginative ID of text (R.id.text in code) and wraps it with a ScrollView in case there are too many events to fit on the screen. The screenshot shows how it looks.

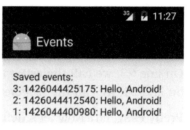

The main program is the onCreate() method in the MainActivity activity. Here's the outline:

eventsv1/src/main/java/org/example/events/MainActivity.java

```
Line 1  package org.example.events;

     -  import static android.provider.BaseColumns._ID;
     -  import static org.example.events.Constants.TABLE_NAME;
     5  import static org.example.events.Constants.TIME;
     -  import static org.example.events.Constants.TITLE;
     -  import android.app.Activity;
     -  import android.content.ContentValues;
     -  import android.database.Cursor;
    10  import android.database.sqlite.SQLiteDatabase;
     -  import android.os.Bundle;
     -  import android.widget.TextView;

     -  public class MainActivity extends Activity {
    15      private EventsData events;
     -      @Override
     -      public void onCreate(Bundle savedInstanceState) {
     -          super.onCreate(savedInstanceState);
     -          setContentView(R.layout.activity_main);
    20          events = new EventsData(this);
     -          try {
     -              addEvent("Hello, Android!");
     -              Cursor cursor = getEvents();
     -              showEvents(cursor);
    25          } finally {
     -              events.close();
     -          }
     -      }
     -  }
```

On line 19 of onCreate(), we set the layout for this view. Then we create an instance of the EventsData class on line 20 and start a try block. If you look ahead to line 26, you can see we close the database inside the finally block. So even if an error occurs in the middle, the database will still be closed.

The events table wouldn't be very interesting if there weren't any events, so on line 22 we call the addEvent() method to add an event to it. Every time you run this program, you'll get a new event. You could add menus or gestures or keystrokes to generate other events if you like, but I'll leave that as an exercise to the reader.

On line 23, we call the getEvents() method to get the list of events, and finally on line 24, we call the showEvents() method to display the list to the user.

Pretty easy, eh? Now let's define those new methods we just used.

Adding a Row

The addEvent() method puts a new record in the database using the string provided as the event title.

```
eventsv1/src/main/java/org/example/events/MainActivity.java
private void addEvent(String string) {
    // Insert a new record into the Events data source.
    // You would do something similar for delete and update.
    SQLiteDatabase db = events.getWritableDatabase();
    ContentValues values = new ContentValues();
    values.put(TIME, System.currentTimeMillis());
    values.put(TITLE, string);
    db.insertOrThrow(TABLE_NAME, null, values);
}
```

Since we need to modify the data, we call getWritableDatabase() to get a read/write handle to the events database. The database handle is cached, so you can call this method as many times as you like.

Next we fill in a ContentValues object with the current time and the event title and pass that to the insertOrThrow() method to do the actual INSERT SQL statement. You don't need to pass in the record ID because SQLite will make one up and return it from the method call.

As the name implies, insertOrThrow() can throw an exception (of type SQLException) if it fails. It doesn't have to be declared with a throws keyword because it's a RuntimeException and not a checked exception. However, if you want to, you can still handle it in a try/catch block like any other exception. If you don't handle it and there's an error, the program will terminate, and a traceback will be dumped to the Android log.

By default, as soon as you do the insert, the database is updated. If you need to batch up or delay modifications for some reason, consult the SQLite website for more details.

Running a Query

The getEvents() method does the database query to get a list of events:

```
eventsv1/src/main/java/org/example/events/MainActivity.java
private static String[] FROM = { _ID, TIME, TITLE, };
private static String ORDER_BY = TIME + " DESC";
private Cursor getEvents() {
    // Perform a managed query. The Activity will handle closing
    // and re-querying the cursor when needed.
    SQLiteDatabase db = events.getReadableDatabase();
    Cursor cursor = db.query(TABLE_NAME, FROM, null, null, null,
            null, ORDER_BY);
    startManagingCursor(cursor);
    return cursor;
}
```

We don't need to modify the database for a query, so we call getReadableDatabase() to get a read-only handle. Then we call query() to perform the actual SELECT SQL statement. FROM is an array of the columns we want, and ORDER_BY tells SQLite to return the results in order from newest to oldest.

Although we don't use them in this example, the query() method has parameters to specify a WHERE clause, a GROUP BY clause, and a HAVING clause. Actually, query() is just a convenience for the programmer. If you prefer, you could build up the SELECT statement yourself in a string and use the rawQuery() method to execute it. Either way, the return value is a Cursor object that represents the result set.

A Cursor is similar to a Java Iterator or a JDBC ResultSet. You call methods on it to get information about the current row, and then you call another method to move to the next row. You'll see how to use it when we display the results in a moment.

The final step is to call startManagingCursor(), which tells the activity to take care of managing the cursor's life cycle based on the activity's life cycle. For example, when the activity is paused, it will automatically deactivate the cursor and then requery it when the activity is restarted. When the activity terminates, all managed cursors will be closed.

Note that startManagingCursor() has been deprecated in later versions of Android. It still works, but there's a better way. We'll cover that in *Using Loaders*, on page 200.

Displaying the Query Results

The last method we need to define is showEvents(). This function takes a Cursor as input and formats the output so the user can read it.

```
eventsv1/src/main/java/org/example/events/MainActivity.java
Line 1  private void showEvents(Cursor cursor) {
    -       // Stuff them all into a big string
    -       StringBuilder builder = new StringBuilder(
    -           "Saved events:\n");
    5       while (cursor.moveToNext()) {
    -           // Could use getColumnIndexOrThrow() to get indexes
    -           long id = cursor.getLong(0);
    -           long time = cursor.getLong(1);
    -           String title = cursor.getString(2);
    10          builder.append(id).append(": ");
    -           builder.append(time).append(": ");
    -           builder.append(title).append("\n");
    -       }
    -       // Display on the screen
    15      TextView text = (TextView) findViewById(R.id.text);
    -       text.setText(builder);
    -   }
```

In this version of Events, we're just going to create a big string (see line 3) to hold all the events items, separated by newlines. This isn't the recommended way to do things, but it'll work for now.

Line 5 calls the Cursor.moveToNext() method to advance to the next row in the data set. When you first get a Cursor, it's positioned before the first record, so calling moveToNext() gets you to the first record. We keep looping until move-ToNext() returns false, which indicates there are no more rows.

Inside the loop (line 7), we call getLong() and getString() to fetch data from the columns of interest, and then we append the values to the string (line 10). There's another method on Cursor, getColumnIndexOrThrow(), that we could've used to get the column index numbers (the values 0, 1, and 2 passed to getLong() and getString()). However, it's a little slow, so if you need it, you should call it outside the loop and remember the indexes yourself.

Once all the rows have been processed, we look up the TextView from layout/activity_main.xml and stuff the big string into it (line 15).

If you run the example now, you should see something like our initial screenshot on page 189. Congratulations on your first Android database program! There's plenty of room for improvement, though.

What would happen if there were thousands or millions of events in the list? The program would be very slow and might run out of memory trying to build a string to hold them all. What if you wanted to let the user select one event and do something with it? If everything is in a string, you can't do that. Luckily, Android provides a better way: data binding.

Data Binding

Data binding allows you to connect your model (data) to your view with just a few lines of code. To demonstrate data binding, we'll modify the Events example to use a ListView that's bound to the result of a database query. First, we need to make the MainActivity class extend ListActivity instead of Activity:

```
eventsv2/src/main/java/org/example/events/MainActivity.java
import android.app.ListActivity;
// ...
public class MainActivity extends ListActivity {
    // ...
}
```

Next, we need to change how the events are displayed in the MainActivity.show-Events() method:

```
eventsv2/src/main/java/org/example/events/MainActivity.java
import android.widget.SimpleCursorAdapter;
// ...
    private static int[] TO = { R.id.rowid, R.id.time, R.id.title, };
    private void showEvents(Cursor cursor) {
        // Set up data binding
        SimpleCursorAdapter adapter = new SimpleCursorAdapter(this,
                R.layout.item, cursor, FROM, TO);
        setListAdapter(adapter);
    }
```

Notice this code is much smaller than before (two lines vs. ten). The first line creates a SimpleCursorAdapter for the Cursor, and the second line tells the ListActivity to use the new adapter. The adapter acts as a go-between, connecting the view with its data source.

If you recall, we first used an adapter in the Suggest sample program on page 155. In that example, we used an ArrayAdapter because the data source was an array defined in XML. For this one, we use a SimpleCursorAdapter because the data source is a Cursor object that came from a database query.

The constructor for SimpleCursorAdapter takes five parameters:

- *context*: A reference to the current Activity
- *layout*: A resource that defines the views for a single list item

- *cursor*: The data set cursor
- *from*: The list of column names where the data is coming from
- *to*: The list of views where the data is going to

The method is deprecated in newer versions of Android, though it continues to work. We'll explore a replacement later in this chapter.

The layout for a list item is defined in layout/item.xml. Note the definitions for the row ID, time, and title views that are referenced in the TO array.

eventsv2/src/main/res/layout/item.xml
```xml
<?xml version="1.0" encoding="utf-8"?>
<RelativeLayout
    xmlns:android="http://schemas.android.com/apk/res/android"
    android:layout_width="fill_parent"
    android:layout_height="fill_parent"
    android:orientation="horizontal"
    android:padding="10sp">
    <TextView
        android:id="@+id/rowid"
        android:layout_width="wrap_content"
        android:layout_height="wrap_content" />
    <TextView
        android:id="@+id/rowidcolon"
        android:layout_width="wrap_content"
        android:layout_height="wrap_content"
        android:text=": "
        android:layout_toRightOf="@id/rowid" />
    <TextView
        android:id="@+id/time"
        android:layout_width="wrap_content"
        android:layout_height="wrap_content"
        android:layout_toRightOf="@id/rowidcolon" />
    <TextView
        android:id="@+id/timecolon"
        android:layout_width="wrap_content"
        android:layout_height="wrap_content"
        android:text=": "
        android:layout_toRightOf="@id/time" />
    <TextView
        android:id="@+id/title"
        android:layout_width="fill_parent"
        android:layout_height="wrap_content"
        android:ellipsize="end"
        android:singleLine="true"
        android:textStyle="italic"
        android:layout_toRightOf="@id/timecolon" />
</RelativeLayout>
```

This looks more complicated than it is. All we're doing is putting the ID, time, and title on one line with colons in between the fields. I added a little padding and formatting to make it look nice.

Finally, we need to change the layout for the activity itself in layout/activity_main.xml. Here's the new version:

```
eventsv2/src/main/res/layout/activity_main.xml
<?xml version="1.0" encoding="utf-8"?>
<LinearLayout
    xmlns:android="http://schemas.android.com/apk/res/android"
    android:layout_width="fill_parent"
    android:layout_height="fill_parent">
    <!-- Note built-in ids for 'list' and 'empty' -->
    <ListView
        android:id="@android:id/list"
        android:layout_width="wrap_content"
        android:layout_height="wrap_content"/>
    <TextView
        android:id="@android:id/empty"
        android:layout_width="wrap_content"
        android:layout_height="wrap_content"
        android:text="@string/empty" />
</LinearLayout>
```

Because the activity extends ListActivity, Android looks for two special ids in the layout file. If the list has items in it, the android:id/list view will be displayed; otherwise, the android:id/empty view will be displayed. So if there are no items, instead of a blank screen the user will see the message "No events!"

Here are the string resources we need:

```
eventsv2/src/main/res/values/strings.xml
<?xml version="1.0" encoding="utf-8"?>
<resources>
    <string name="app_name">Events</string>
    <string name="action_settings">Settings</string>
    <string name="empty">No events!</string>
</resources>
```

The final result is shown in the figure on page 196.

As an exercise for the reader, think about how you could enhance this application now that you have a real list to play with. For example, when the user selects an event, you could open a detail viewer, mail the event to technical support, or perhaps delete the selected event and all the ones below it from the database.

Figure 7—The final result. using ListActivity and data binding.

There's still one little problem with this example. No other application can add things to the events database or even look at them! For that, we need to use an Android ContentProvider.

Using a ContentProvider

In the Android security model (see the discussion in *Safe and Secure*, on page 26), files written by one application cannot be read from or written to by any other application. Each program has its own Linux user ID and data directory (/data/data/*packagename*) and its own protected memory space. Android programs can communicate with each other in two ways:

- *Inter-Process Communication (IPC)*: One process declares an arbitrary API using the Android Interface Definition Language (AIDL) and the IBinder interface. Parameters are marshaled safely and efficiently between processes when the API is called. This advanced technique is used for remote procedure calls to a background Service thread. IPC, services, and binders are beyond the scope of this book. For more information, see the online documentation for aidl,[3] Service,[4] and IBinder.[5]

- *ContentProvider*: Processes register themselves to the system as providers of certain kinds of data. When that information is requested, they're called by Android through a fixed API to query or modify the content in whatever way they see fit. This is the technique we're going to use for the Events sample.

---

3.   http://d.android.com/guide/components/aidl.html
4.   http://d.android.com/reference/android/app/Service.html
5.   http://d.android.com/reference/android/os/IBinder.html

Any piece of information managed by a ContentProvider is addressed through a URI that looks like this:

content://*authority*/*path*/*id*

where:

- content:// is the standard required prefix.

- *authority* is the name of the provider. Using your fully qualified package name is recommended to prevent name collisions.

- *path* is a virtual directory within the provider that identifies the kind of data being requested.

- *id* is the primary key of a specific record being requested. To request all records of a particular type, omit this and the trailing slash.

Android comes with several providers already built in, including the following:

- content://browser
- content://contacts
- content://media
- content://settings

For an up-to-date list, see the online doc.[6] Instead of using the strings here, use the documented constants such as Browser.BOOKMARKS_URI. Note that access to some providers requires additional permissions to be requested in your manifest file.

To demonstrate using a ContentProvider, let's convert the Events example to use one. For our Events provider, these will be valid URIs:

```
content://org.example.events/events/3  -- single event with _id=3
content://org.example.events/events  -- all events
```

First we need to add two more constants to Constants.java:

```
eventsv3/src/main/java/org/example/events/Constants.java
import android.net.Uri;
// ...
    public static final String AUTHORITY = "org.example.events";
    public static final Uri CONTENT_URI = Uri.parse("content://"
        + AUTHORITY + "/" + TABLE_NAME);
```

The layout files (activity_main.xml and item.xml) don't need to be changed, so the next step is to make a few minor changes to the MainActivity class.

---

6.   http://d.android.com/reference/android/provider/package-summary.html

Changing the Main Program

The main program (the MainActivity.onCreate() method) actually gets a little simpler because there's no database object to keep track of:

eventsv3/src/main/java/org/example/events/MainActivity.java

```
@Override
public void onCreate(Bundle savedInstanceState) {
    super.onCreate(savedInstanceState);
    setContentView(R.layout.activity_main);
    addEvent("Hello, Android!");
    Cursor cursor = getEvents();
    showEvents(cursor);
}
```

We don't need the try/finally block, and we can remove references to EventData.

Adding a Row

Two lines change in addEvent(). Here's the new version:

eventsv3/src/main/java/org/example/events/MainActivity.java

```
import static org.example.events.Constants.CONTENT_URI;
// ...
    private void addEvent(String string) {
        // Insert a new record into the Events data source.
        // You would do something similar for delete and update.
        ContentValues values = new ContentValues();
        values.put(TIME, System.currentTimeMillis());
        values.put(TITLE, string);
        getContentResolver().insert(CONTENT_URI, values);
    }
```

The call to getWritableDatabase() is gone, and the call to insertOrThrow() is replaced by getContentResolver().insert(). Instead of a database handle, we use a content URI.

Running a Query

The getEvents() method is also simplified when using a ContentProvider:

eventsv3/src/main/java/org/example/events/MainActivity.java

```
private Cursor getEvents() {
    // Perform a managed query. The Activity will handle closing
    // and re-querying the cursor when needed.
    return managedQuery(CONTENT_URI, FROM, null, null, ORDER_BY);
}
```

Here we use the Activity.managedQuery() method, passing it the content URI, the list of columns we're interested in, and the order they should be sorted in.

By removing all references to the database, we've decoupled the Events client from the Events data provider. The client is simpler, but now we have to implement a new piece we didn't have before.

Implementing a ContentProvider

A ContentProvider is a high-level object like an Activity that needs to be declared to the system. So, the first step when making one is to add it to your Android-Manifest.xml file before the <activity> tag (as a child of <application>):

eventsv3/src/main/AndroidManifest.xml
```xml
<provider
        android:name=".EventsProvider"
        android:authorities="org.example.events"/>
```

android:name is the class name (appended to the manifest's package name), and android:authorities is the string used in the content URI.

Next we create the EventsProvider class, which must extend ContentProvider. Here's the basic outline:

eventsv3/src/main/java/org/example/events/EventsProvider.java
```java
package org.example.events;

import static android.provider.BaseColumns._ID;
import static org.example.events.Constants.AUTHORITY;
import static org.example.events.Constants.CONTENT_URI;
import static org.example.events.Constants.TABLE_NAME;
import android.content.ContentProvider;
import android.content.ContentUris;
import android.content.ContentValues;
import android.content.UriMatcher;
import android.database.Cursor;
import android.database.sqlite.SQLiteDatabase;
import android.net.Uri;
import android.text.TextUtils;

public class EventsProvider extends ContentProvider {
    private static final int EVENTS = 1;
    private static final int EVENTS_ID = 2;

    /** The MIME type of a directory of events */
    private static final String CONTENT_TYPE
        = "vnd.android.cursor.dir/vnd.example.event";

    /** The MIME type of a single event */
    private static final String CONTENT_ITEM_TYPE
        = "vnd.android.cursor.item/vnd.example.event";

    private EventsData events;
```

```
    private UriMatcher uriMatcher;
    // ...
}
```

By convention we use vnd.example instead of org.example in the MIME type. Multipurpose Internet Mail Extensions (MIME) is an Internet standard for describing the type of any kind of content.

EventsProvider handles two types of data:

- EVENTS (MIME type CONTENT_TYPE): A directory or list of events
- EVENTS_ID (MIME type CONTENT_ITEM_TYPE): A single event

In terms of the URI, the difference is that the first type doesn't specify an ID, but the second type does. We use Android's UriMatcher class to parse the URI and tell us which one the client specified. And we reuse the EventsData class from earlier in the chapter to manage the real database inside the provider.

In the interest of space, I'm not going to show the rest of the class here, but you can download the whole thing from the book's website. All the versions of the Events example can be found in the source code Zip file.

The current version of the Events sample looks exactly like the previous version on the outside. On the inside, however, you now have the framework for an event store that can be used by other applications in the system, even ones written by other developers.

Using Loaders

While you were coding the example in this chapter, you may have noticed warnings about managedQuery() and the SimpleCursorAdapter constructor we were using being deprecated. They still work, and many examples you'll find on the web still use them. But current versions of Android provide a much better way of doing long-running operations such as database queries: loaders.

Loaders are preferred for several reasons:

- They provide asynchronous loading of data. managedQuery() puts data loading in the UI thread, which can lead to pauses and stutters in the user interface.

- They monitor the source of the data and deliver results as soon as they're available, without requiring a requery.

- They retain their data across configuration changes, avoiding a requery every time you rotate the screen or pause the app.

Using a loader will require a slight restructuring of our application. Luckily, all the changes are contained in the MainActivity class. First, let's add a few import statements at the top to bring in the classes we need:

eventsv4/src/main/java/org/example/events/MainActivity.java

```
import android.app.LoaderManager;
import android.content.CursorLoader;
import android.content.Loader;
```

Next, change the MainActivity class to implement the LoaderCallbacks interface and declare a couple of extra variables:

eventsv4/src/main/java/org/example/events/MainActivity.java

```
public class MainActivity extends ListActivity implements
        LoaderManager.LoaderCallbacks<Cursor> {
    // ...
    // The loader's unique id (within this activity)
    private final static int LOADER_ID = 1;

    // The adapter that binds our data to the ListView
    private SimpleCursorAdapter mAdapter;
}
```

Then, get rid of the getEvents() and showEvents() methods because we won't need them anymore. Change the onCreate() method as follows:

eventsv4/src/main/java/org/example/events/MainActivity.java

```
@Override
public void onCreate(Bundle savedInstanceState) {
    super.onCreate(savedInstanceState);
    setContentView(R.layout.activity_main);

    // Initialize the adapter. It starts off empty.
    mAdapter = new SimpleCursorAdapter(this, R.layout.item, null, FROM, TO, 0);

    // Associate the adapter with the ListView
    setListAdapter(mAdapter);

    // Initialize the loader
    LoaderManager lm = getLoaderManager();
    lm.initLoader(LOADER_ID, null, this);

    addEvent("Hello, Android!");
}
```

We create the adapter and associate it with the list view in the onCreate() method instead of waiting until later. The adapter starts out empty but later we'll add an event to it with the addEvent() method. Then we'll get a handle to the loader manager and initialize a loader.

The last parameter to the initLoader() method, this, refers to the MainActivity class that we just changed to implement the LoaderCallbacks interface. Therefore, we need to supply the three extra methods required by that interface now:

eventsv4/src/main/java/org/example/events/MainActivity.java

```
@Override
public Loader<Cursor> onCreateLoader(int id, Bundle args) {
    // Create a new CursorLoader
    return new CursorLoader(this, CONTENT_URI, FROM, null, null, ORDER_BY);
}

@Override
public void onLoadFinished(Loader<Cursor> loader, Cursor cursor) {
    switch (loader.getId()) {
        case LOADER_ID:
            // The data is now available to use
            mAdapter.swapCursor(cursor);
            break;
    }
}

@Override
public void onLoaderReset(Loader<Cursor> loader) {
    // The loader's data is unavailable
    mAdapter.swapCursor(null);
}
```

The first method, onCreateLoader(), is called when we need to create a new loader. It just creates a new CursorLoader and returns it.

The onLoadFinished() method is called when the loader finishes filling up the cursor. Once filled, the cursor can be swapped in to the adapter so the adapter (and thus the list it's connected to) will start showing the new data.

Finally, the onLoaderReset() method is called when there's no data in the loader, so we have to swap out the cursor with a null one that contains no data.

When you run the program this time, it looks pretty much the same as before. The app runs too fast to really tell a difference in speed. But take my word for it—moving database queries, network I/O, calculations, and any other time-consuming activities out of the main GUI thread is just what the doctor ordered for creating smooth, stutter-free apps.

Closing Thoughts

In this chapter, you learned how to store data in an Android SQL database. If you want to do more with SQL, you'll need to learn about more statements and expressions than the ones we covered here. A book such as *SQL Pocket*

Guide [Gen10] by Jonathan Gennick or *The Definitive Guide to SQLite [AO10]* by Mike Owens would be a good investment, but keep in mind that the SQL syntax and functions vary slightly from database to database.

The SimpleCursorAdapter introduced in this chapter can be customized to show more than just text. For example, you could display rating stars, sparklines (small graphs), or other views based on data in the Cursor class. For more information, look for ViewBinder in the SimpleCursorAdapter documentation.[7]

Loaders are not the only way to make your apps perform better. In case you missed it, see how we used the Executor and Runnable classes in Chapter 11, *Calling Web Services*, on page 155 to perform network I/O on a separate thread.

This concludes your introduction to Android. To help you on your journey from this point on, be sure to check out the resources and source code at the book's website.[8] You can also find the answers to many of your questions at the Android section of Stack Overflow.[9]

Now go forth and create something great!

---

7. http://d.android.com/reference/android/widget/SimpleCursorAdapter.html
8. http://pragprog.com/book/eband4
9. http://stackoverflow.com/questions/tagged/android

Part V

Appendixes

Java vs. the Android Language and APIs

For the most part, Android programs are written in the Java language, and they use the Java 6 Standard Edition (SE) library APIs. I say "for the most part" because there are a few differences. This appendix highlights the differences between regular Java and what you'll find in Android. ART (the runtime system used for Android 5.0 and above) and Dalvik (the system used prior to Android 5.0) have the same restrictions.

If you're already proficient in Java development on other platforms, you should take a close look to see what things you need to "unlearn."

Language Subset

Android uses a standard Java compiler to compile your source code into regular bytecodes and then translates those bytecodes into instructions to execute. Therefore, nearly the entire Java language is supported, not just a small subset. By using the stock compiler and bytecodes, you often don't even need to have the source code for libraries that you want to use in your applications.

Language Level

Android Studio supports code compatible with Java Standard Edition 6 or earlier, with optional additions from Java 7. At present, none of the Java 8 features are available.

To enable Java 7 language features, you need to add these lines to your gradle build file:

```
compileOptions {
    sourceCompatibility JavaVersion.VERSION_1_7
    targetCompatibility JavaVersion.VERSION_1_7
}
```

This will let you use the following Java 7 language features in apps targeting Android 2.2 (Froyo) and higher:

- Diamond operator (<>)
- String switch
- Multiple-catch (catch (Exc1 | Exc2 e))
- Underscore in number literals (1_234_567)
- Binary literals (0b1110111)

It will also enable these features for Android 4.4 (KitKat) and above:

- The try-with-resources statement
- The @SafeVarargs annotation

Naturally, a Java 7 or higher JDK is needed to unlock all these features.

Intrinsic Types

All Java intrinsic types, including byte, char, short, int, long, float, double, Object, String, and arrays, are supported. On older, low-end hardware, floating-point math may be emulated. That means operations with doubles and floats will be performed in software instead of hardware, making it much slower than integer arithmetic. However, modern Android devices all have good floating-point hardware, so this is unlikely to be a concern.

Multithreading and Synchronization

Multiple threads are supported by *time slicing*: giving each thread a few milliseconds to run and then performing a *context switch* to let another thread have a turn. Although Android will support any number of threads, as a rule of thumb you should limit them to 1 plus the number of cores on the machine. One thread is dedicated for the main user interface (if you have one), and the rest are used for long-running operations such as calculations or network I/O.

For example, if your app is running on a quad-core device, you'll get the best results by limiting your total number of threads to 5. You can use the Runtime.getRuntime().availableProcessors() function to tell how many cores there are.

Android implements the synchronized keyword and synchronization-related library methods such as Object.wait(), Object.notify(), and Object.notifyAll(). It also supports the java.util.concurrent package for more sophisticated algorithms. Use them as you would in any Java program to keep multiple threads from interfering with each other.

Reflection

Although the Android platform supports Java reflection, you may not want to use it, especially in timing sensitive code. The reason is simple performance and power: reflection is slow, and slow code uses more battery power. Consider alternatives such as compile-time tools and preprocessors instead.

Finalization

Android supports object finalization during garbage collection just like regular Java VMs. However, most Java experts advise you not to rely on finalizers because you can't predict when (or if) they'll run. Instead of finalizers, use explicit close() or terminate() methods. Android is targeted toward resource-constrained hardware, so it's important that you release all resources as soon as you no longer need them.

Standard Library Subset

Android supports a relatively large subset of the Java Standard Edition 6.0 library. Some things were left out because they simply didn't make sense, and others were omitted because better APIs are available that are specific to Android. As noted earlier, a few Java 7 features are supported in newer versions of Android starting with Android 4.4 (KitKat), including the AutoClosable interface and @SafeVarargs. In general, though, Java 7 and 8 additions to the library API aren't supported, including the new filesystem API (NIO 2.0), Fork and Join, and invokedynamic.

Supported

The following standard packages are supported in Android. Consult the Java 2 Platform Standard Edition 6.0 API documentation[1] for information on how to use them:

- java.awt.font: A few constants for Unicode and fonts
- java.beans: A few classes and interfaces for JavaBeans property changes
- java.io: File and stream I/O
- java.lang (except java.lang.management): Language and exception support
- java.math: Big numbers, rounding, precision
- java.net: Network I/O, URLs, sockets
- java.nio: File and channel I/O
- java.security: Authorization, certificates, public keys
- java.sql: Database interfaces

---

1.   http://docs.oracle.com/javase/6/docs/api/

- java.text: Formatting, natural language, collation
- java.util (including java.util.concurrent): Lists, maps, sets, arrays, collections
- javax.crypto: Ciphers, public keys
- javax.microedition.khronos: OpenGL graphics (from Java Micro Edition)
- javax.net: Socket factories, SSL
- javax.security (except javax.security.auth.kerberos, javax.security.auth.spi, and javax.security.sasl)
- javax.sql (except javax.sql.rowset): More database interfaces
- javax.xml.parsers: XML parsing
- org.w3c.dom (but not subpackages): DOM nodes and elements
- org.xml.sax: Simple API for XML

Note that although the regular Java SQL database APIs (JDBC) are included, you don't use them to access local SQLite databases. Use the android.database APIs instead (see Chapter 13, *Putting SQL to Work*, on page 183).

Not Supported

These packages, normally part of the Java 2 Platform Standard Edition, are *not* supported by Android:

- java.applet
- java.awt
- java.lang.management
- java.rmi
- javax.accessibility
- javax.activity
- javax.imageio
- javax.management
- javax.naming
- javax.print
- javax.rmi
- javax.security.auth.kerberos
- javax.security.auth.spi
- javax.security.sasl
- javax.sound
- javax.swing
- javax.transaction
- javax.xml (except javax.xml.parsers)
- org.ietf.*
- org.omg.*
- org.w3c.dom.* (subpackages)

Third-Party Libraries

In addition to the standard libraries listed earlier, the Android SDK comes with several third-party libraries for your convenience:

- org.json: JavaScript Object Notation
- org.xml.sax: XML parsing
- org.xmlpull.v1: XML parsing

Bibliography

[AGH05] Ken Arnold, James Gosling, and David Holmes. *The Java Programming Language*. Prentice Hall, Englewood Cliffs, NJ, 4th, 2005.

[AO10]   Grant Allen and Mike Owens. *The Definitive Guide to SQLite*. Apress, New York City, NY, 2nd, 2010.

[Blo08] Joshua Bloch. *Effective Java*. Addison-Wesley, Reading, MA, 2008.

[EF14]   Ben Evans and David Flanagan. *Java In A Nutshell*. O'Reilly & Associates, Inc., Sebastopol, CA, 6th, 2014.

[Gen10] Jonathan Gennick. *SQL Pocket Guide*. O'Reilly & Associates, Inc., Sebastopol, CA, 3rd, 2010.

[Goe06] Brian Goetz. *Java Concurrency in Practice*. Addison-Wesley, Reading, MA, 2006.

[HT99]   Andrew Hunt and David Thomas. *The Pragmatic Programmer*. The Pragmatic Bookshelf, Raleigh, NC and Dallas, TX, 1999.

[JT95]   Ollie Johnston and Frank Thomas. *The Illusion of Life: Disney Animation*. Disney Editions, New York City, NY, Rev Sub, 1995.

[SB05]   Kathy Sierra and Bert Bates. *Head First Java*. O'Reilly & Associates, Inc., Sebastopol, CA, 2nd, 2005.

[Ses05] Peter Sestoft. *Java Precisely*. MIT Press, Cambridge, MA, 2nd, 2005.

Index

Android and Processing

Script your Android device right on the device, and explore Processing on Android for faster development.

Developing Android on Android

Take advantage of the open, tinker-friendly Android platform and make your device work the way you want it to. Quickly create Android tasks, scripts, and programs entirely on your Android device—no PC required. Learn how to build your own innovative Android programs and workflows with tools you can run on Android itself, and tailor the Android default user interface to match your mobile lifestyle needs. Apply your favorite scripting language to rapidly develop programs that speak the time and battery level, alert you to important events or locations, read your new email to you, and much more.

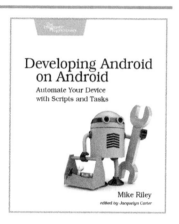

Mike Riley
(232 pages) ISBN: 9781937785543. $36
https://pragprog.com/book/mrand

Rapid Android Development

Create mobile apps for Android phones and tablets faster and more easily than you ever imagined. Use "Processing," the free, award-winning, graphics-savvy language and development environment, to work with the touchscreens, hardware sensors, cameras, network transceivers, and other devices and software in the latest Android phones and tablets.

Daniel Sauter
(392 pages) ISBN: 9781937785062. $33
https://pragprog.com/book/dsproc

Seven in Seven

From Web Frameworks to Concurrency Models, see what the rest of the world is doing with this introduction to seven different approaches.

Seven Web Frameworks in Seven Weeks

Whether you need a new tool or just inspiration, *Seven Web Frameworks in Seven Weeks* explores modern options, giving you a taste of each with ideas that will help you create better apps. You'll see frameworks that leverage modern programming languages, employ unique architectures, live client-side instead of server-side, or embrace type systems. You'll see everything from familiar Ruby and JavaScript to the more exotic Erlang, Haskell, and Clojure.

Jack Moffitt, Fred Daoud
(302 pages) ISBN: 9781937785635. $38
https://pragprog.com/book/7web

Seven Concurrency Models in Seven Weeks

Your software needs to leverage multiple cores, handle thousands of users and terabytes of data, and continue working in the face of both hardware and software failure. Concurrency and parallelism are the keys, and *Seven Concurrency Models in Seven Weeks* equips you for this new world. See how emerging technologies such as actors and functional programming address issues with traditional threads and locks development. Learn how to exploit the parallelism in your computer's GPU and leverage clusters of machines with MapReduce and Stream Processing. And do it all with the confidence that comes from using tools that help you write crystal clear, high-quality code.

Paul Butcher
(296 pages) ISBN: 9781937785659. $38
https://pragprog.com/book/pb7con

Be Agile

Don't just "do" agile; you want to *be* agile. We'll show you how, for new code and old.

Your Code as a Crime Scene

Jack the Ripper and legacy codebases have more in common than you'd think. Inspired by forensic psychology methods, this book teaches you strategies to predict the future of your codebase, assess refactoring direction, and understand how your team influences the design. With its unique blend of forensic psychology and code analysis, this book arms you with the strategies you need, no matter what programming language you use.

Adam Tornhill
(218 pages) ISBN: 9781680500387. $36
https://pragprog.com/book/atcrime

The Nature of Software Development

You need to get value from your software project. You need it "free, now, and perfect." We can't get you there, but we can help you get to "cheaper, sooner, and better." This book leads you from the desire for value down to the specific activities that help good Agile projects deliver better software sooner, and at a lower cost. Using simple sketches and a few words, the author invites you to follow his path of learning and understanding from a half century of software development and from his engagement with Agile methods from their very beginning.

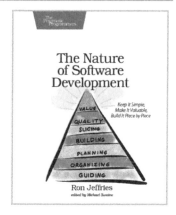

Ron Jeffries
(178 pages) ISBN: 9781941222379. $24
https://pragprog.com/book/rjnsd

Long Live the Command Line!

Use tmux and Vim for incredible mouse-free productivity.

tmux

Your mouse is slowing you down. The time you spend context switching between your editor and your consoles eats away at your productivity. Take control of your environment with tmux, a terminal multiplexer that you can tailor to your workflow. Learn how to customize, script, and leverage tmux's unique abilities and keep your fingers on your keyboard's home row.

Brian P. Hogan
(88 pages) ISBN: 9781934356968. $16.25
https://pragprog.com/book/bhtmux

Practical Vim

Vim is a fast and efficient text editor that will make you a faster and more efficient developer. It's available on almost every OS—if you master the techniques in this book, you'll never need another text editor. In more than 100 Vim tips, you'll quickly learn the editor's core functionality and tackle your trickiest editing and writing tasks.

Drew Neil
(346 pages) ISBN: 9781934356982. $29
https://pragprog.com/book/dnvim

Past and Present

To see where we're going, remember how we got here, and learn how to take a healthier approach to programming.

Fire in the Valley

In the 1970s, while their contemporaries were protesting the computer as a tool of dehumanization and oppression, a motley collection of college dropouts, hippies, and electronics fanatics were engaged in something much more subversive. Obsessed with the idea of getting computer power into their own hands, they launched from their garages a hobbyist movement that grew into an industry, and ultimately a social and technological revolution. What they did was invent the personal computer: not just a new device, but a watershed in the relationship between man and machine. This is their story.

Michael Swaine and Paul Freiberger
(424 pages) ISBN: 9781937785765. $34
https://pragprog.com/book/fsfire

The Healthy Programmer

To keep doing what you love, you need to maintain your own systems, not just the ones you write code for. Regular exercise and proper nutrition help you learn, remember, concentrate, and be creative—skills critical to doing your job well. Learn how to change your work habits, master exercises that make working at a computer more comfortable, and develop a plan to keep fit, healthy, and sharp for years to come.

This book is intended only as an informative guide for those wishing to know more about health issues. In no way is this book intended to replace, countermand, or conflict with the advice given to you by your own healthcare provider including Physician, Nurse Practitioner, Physician Assistant, Registered Dietician, and other licensed professionals.

Joe Kutner
(254 pages) ISBN: 9781937785314. $36
https://pragprog.com/book/jkthp

The Pragmatic Bookshelf

The Pragmatic Bookshelf features books written by developers for developers. The titles continue the well-known Pragmatic Programmer style and continue to garner awards and rave reviews. As development gets more and more difficult, the Pragmatic Programmers will be there with more titles and products to help you stay on top of your game.

Visit Us Online

This Book's Home Page
https://pragprog.com/book/eband4
Source code from this book, errata, and other resources. Come give us feedback, too!

Register for Updates
https://pragprog.com/updates
Be notified when updates and new books become available.

Join the Community
https://pragprog.com/community
Read our weblogs, join our online discussions, participate in our mailing list, interact with our wiki, and benefit from the experience of other Pragmatic Programmers.

New and Noteworthy
https://pragprog.com/news
Check out the latest pragmatic developments, new titles and other offerings.

Save on the eBook

Save on the eBook versions of this title. Owning the paper version of this book entitles you to purchase the electronic versions at a terrific discount.

PDFs are great for carrying around on your laptop—they are hyperlinked, have color, and are fully searchable. Most titles are also available for the iPhone and iPod touch, Amazon Kindle, and other popular e-book readers.

Buy now at *https://pragprog.com/coupon*

Contact Us

Online Orders:	*https://pragprog.com/catalog*
Customer Service:	*support@pragprog.com*
International Rights:	*translations@pragprog.com*
Academic Use:	*academic@pragprog.com*
Write for Us:	*http://write-for-us.pragprog.com*
Or Call:	+1 800-699-7764

CPSIA information can be obtained at www.ICGtesting.com
Printed in the USA
BVOW10s1827100515

399685BV00003B/4/P